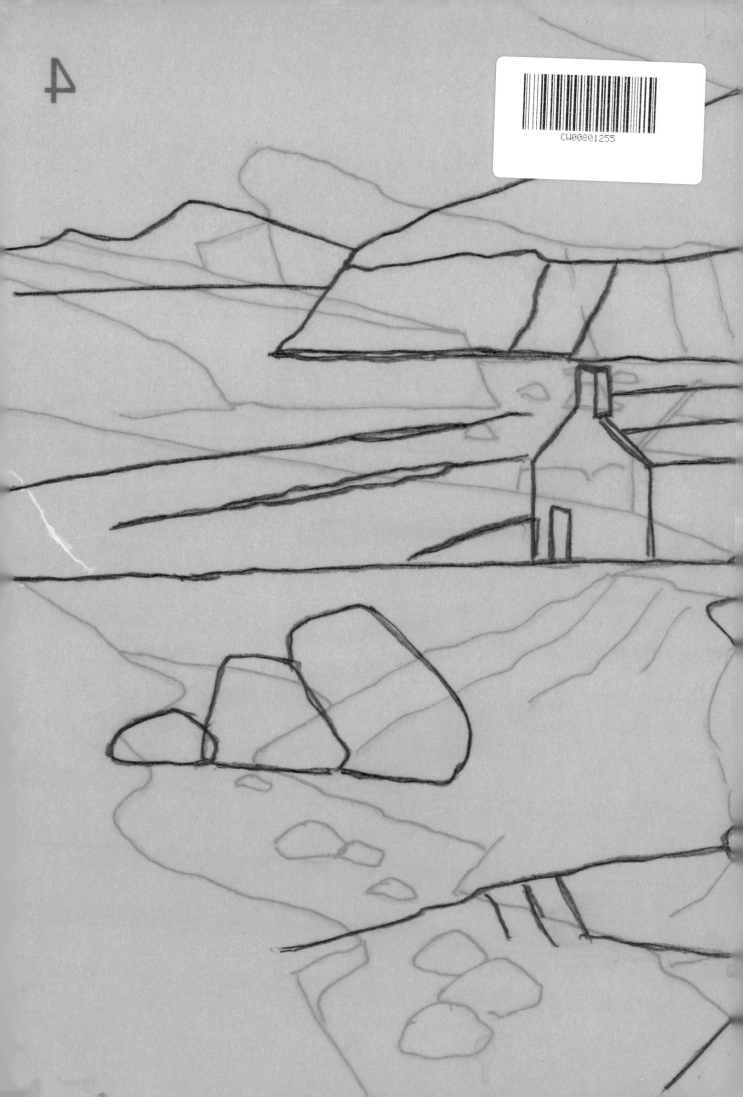

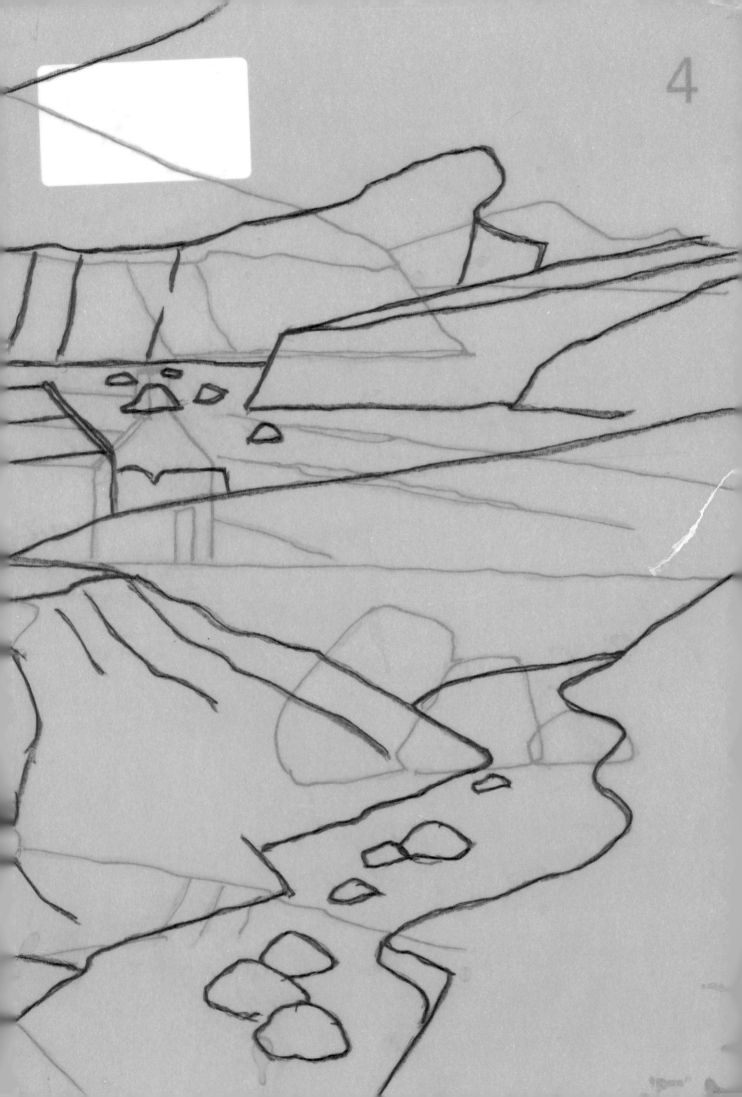

4

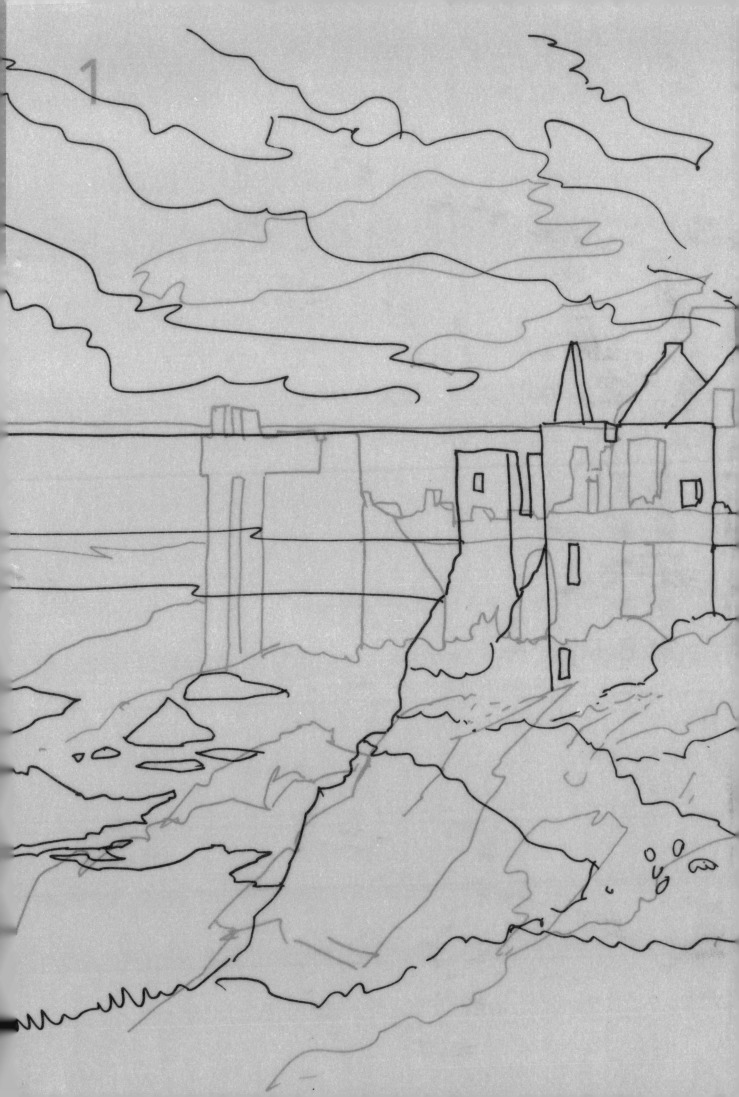

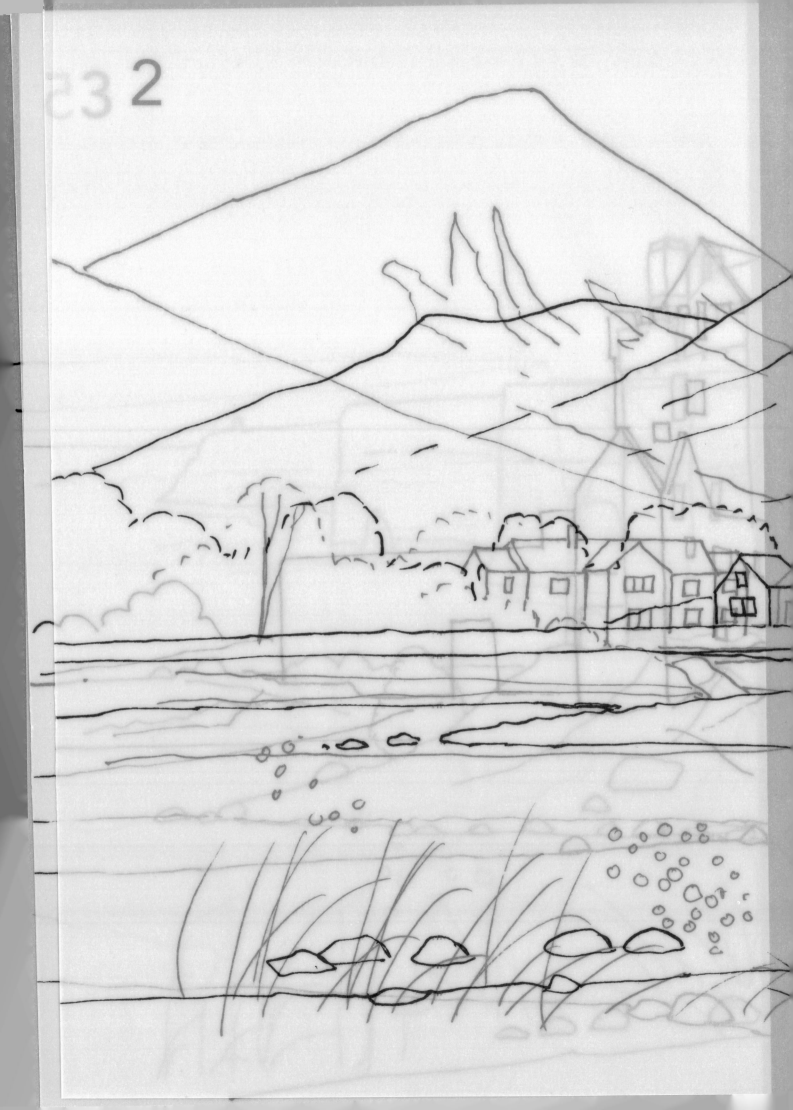

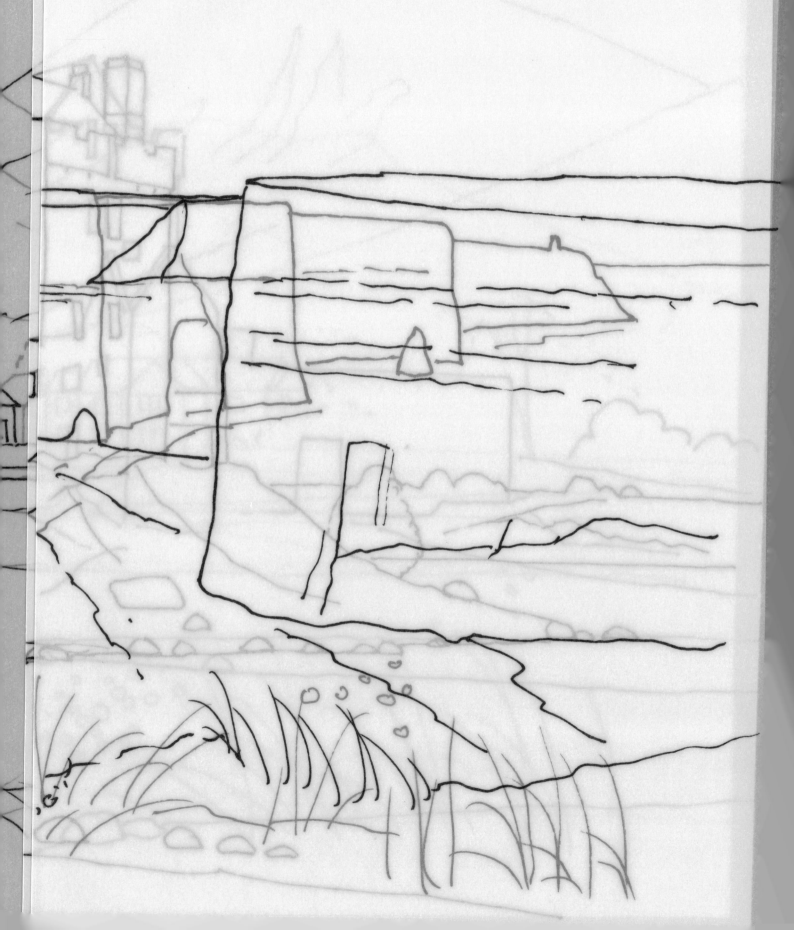

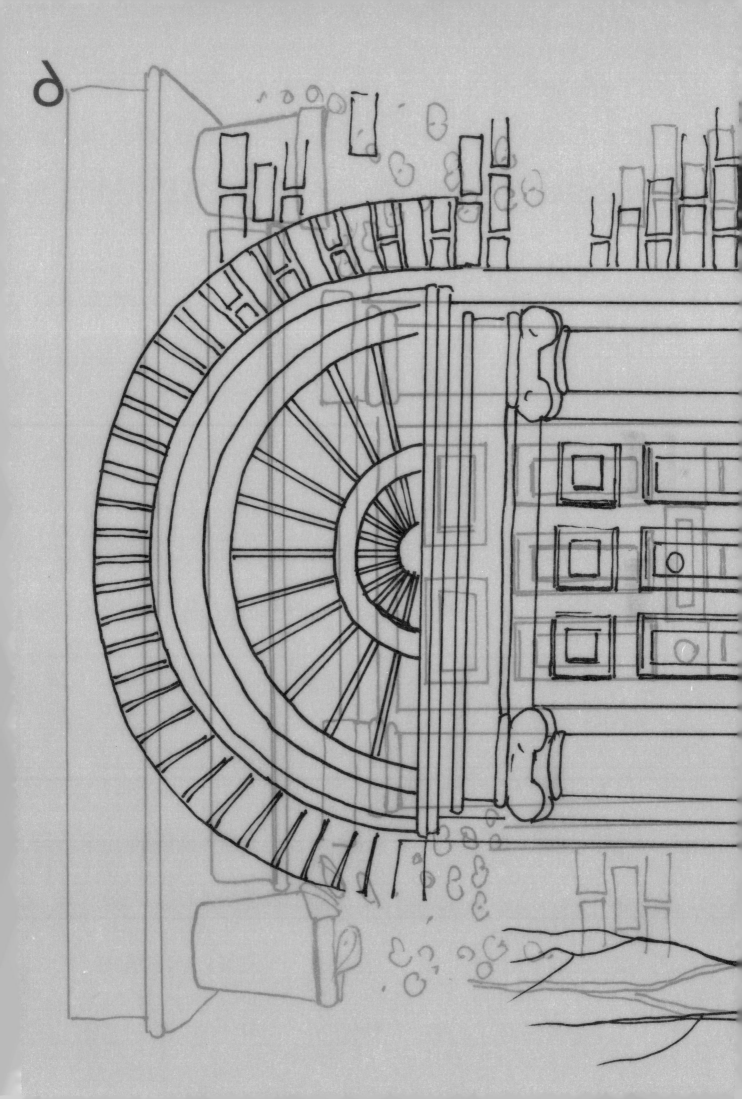

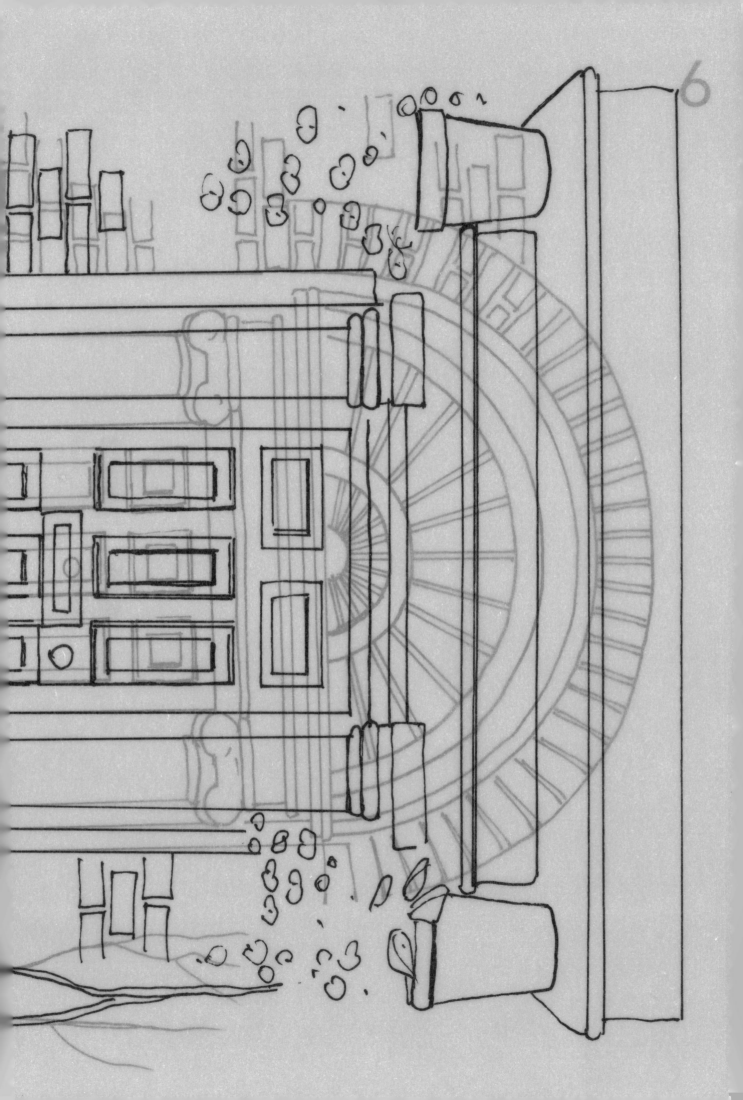

6

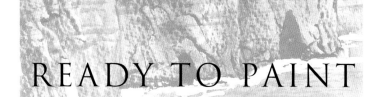

READY TO PAINT

Ireland
in Watercolour

Terry Harrison

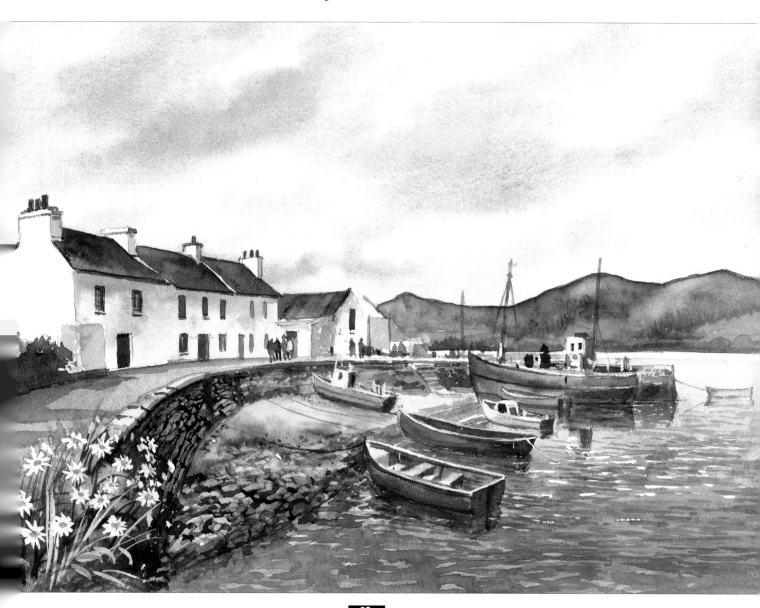

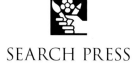

SEARCH PRESS

First published in Great Britain 2009

Search Press Limited
Wellwood, North Farm Road,
Tunbridge Wells, Kent TN2 3DR

ISBN: 978-1-84448-363-1

The Publishers and author can accept no responsibility for any
consequences arising from the information, advice or instructions given
in this publication.

Readers are permitted to reproduce any of the tracings or paintings in
this book for their personal use, or for the purposes of selling for charity,
free of charge and without the prior permission of the Publishers.
Any use of the tracings or paintings for commercial purposes is not
permitted without the prior permission of the Publishers.

Suppliers
If you have any difficulty obtaining any of the materials and equipment
mentioned in this book, please visit the Search Press website:
www.searchpress.com

For more information, contact Terry Harrison at:
Telephone: +44 (0)1386 584840
Website: terryharrison.com

Publisher's note
All the step-by-step photographs in this book feature the author,
Terry Harrison, demonstrating watercolour painting techniques.
No models have been used.

Please note that when removing the perforated sheets of tracing paper
from the book, score them first, then carefully pull out each sheet.

Printed in China

Dedicated to Fiona Peart.

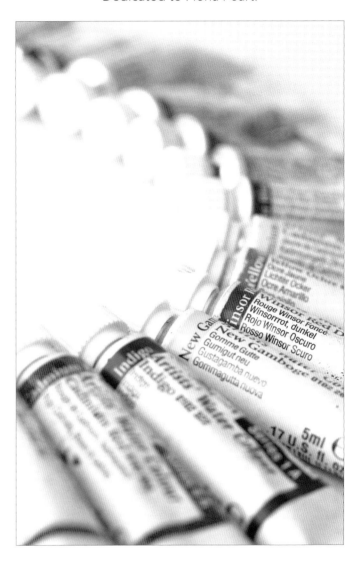

Page 1

Sweeney's Quay, County Mayo
40 x 28cm (15¾ x 11in)

*This quaint little quay in the west of Ireland is such a typical Irish
scene. Whitewashed cottages on the quayside, colourful boats in the
harbour and the distant hills of Achill Island over the water make
this an irresistible subject to paint.*

Opposite

Fitzgerald's, Avoca, County Wicklow
40 x 28cm (15¾ x 11in)

*Avoca is the village where the BBC series **Ballykissangel** was filmed.
There are many iconic images associated with Ireland, and one is
a traditional Irish pub. What I love about this scene are the three
locals: two of them are putting the world to rights over a pint of
the 'black stuff' and the other is savouring a well-earned rest from
walking the dog.*

Contents

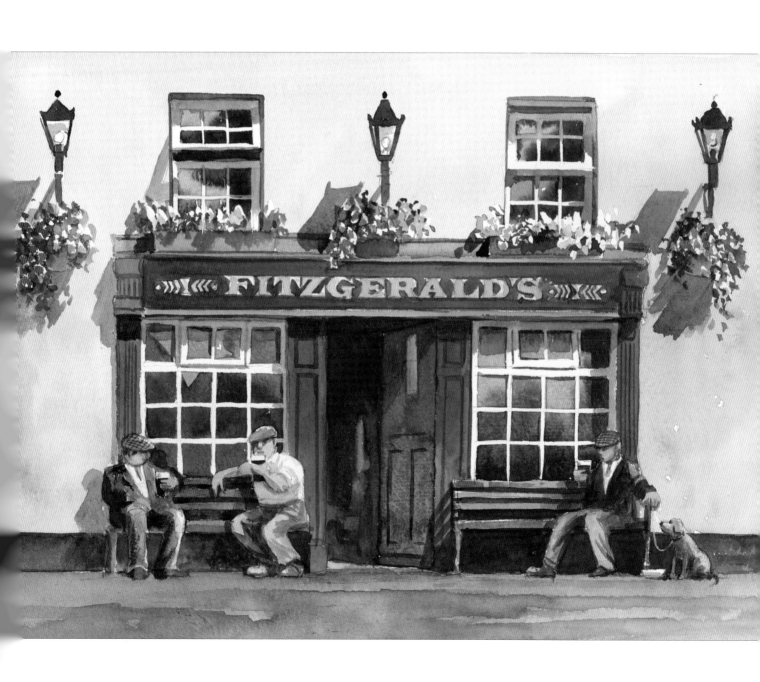

Introduction

Ireland has so much heritage and breathtaking beauty that to choose just five different painting projects which capture the essence of the country was quite a challenge. I think this selection just scratches the surface.

The first thing that strikes you about Ireland is how green it is – no wonder they call it the Emerald Isle. I have tried to capture the heritage, beauty and spirit of Ireland with its rugged coastline, mystical mountains and crumbling castles. Perhaps it is the locals, well known for their creativity and good humour, who make Ireland so inspiring; whatever the reason, there is something about the country that makes you want to paint it.

With the help of the tracing paper outlines and the step-by-step instructions, I can help you to achieve paintings which capture the stunning scenery and history of this enchanting isle without the need for drawing.

TRACING

1

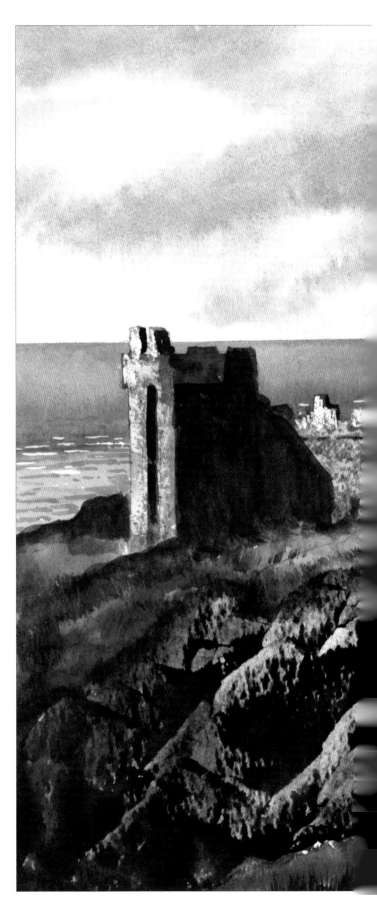

Dunluce Castle, North Antrim
42 x 29cm (16½ x 11½in)

This castle is situated on the North Antrim coast and is perched majestically on the edge of a basalt outcrop, connected to the mainland by an arched bridge. The castle is dramatically surrounded by terrifying steep drops. If you were looking for a site for a castle, you would be hard pushed to beat this place. The tracing for this painting is available to pull out at the front of this book.

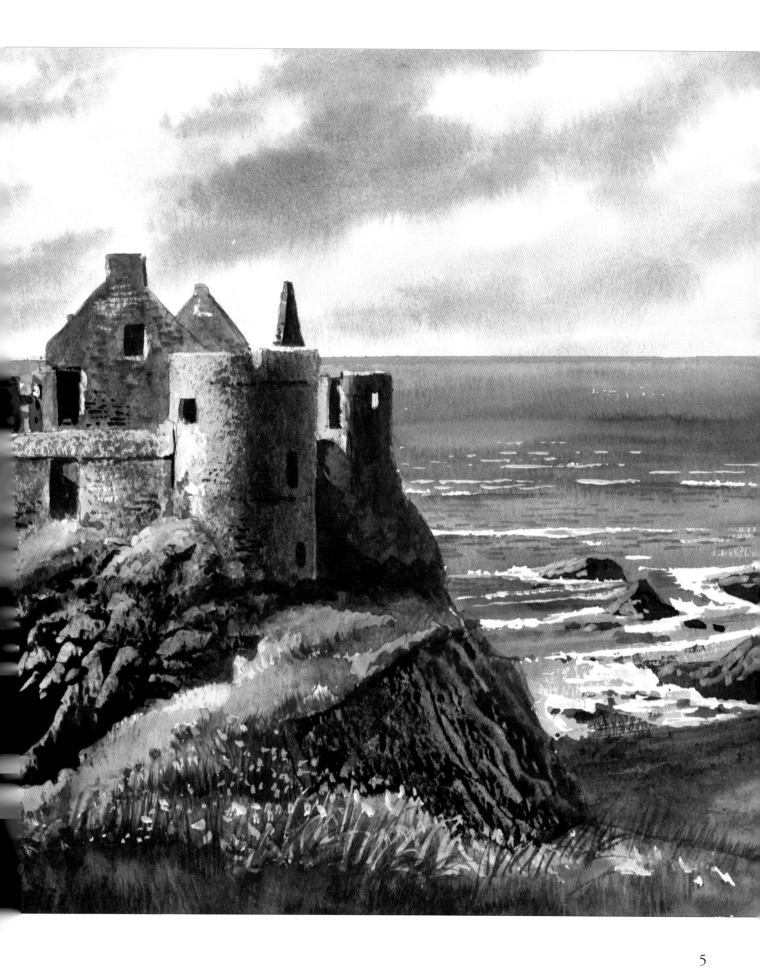

Materials

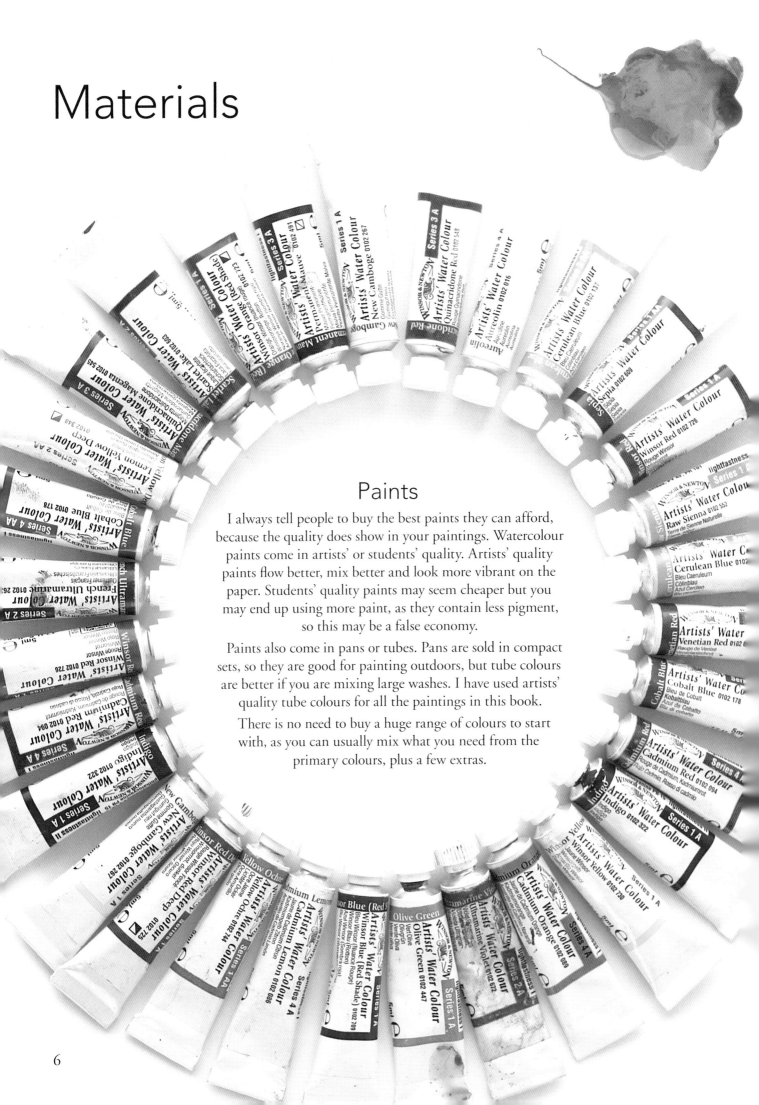

Paints

I always tell people to buy the best paints they can afford, because the quality does show in your paintings. Watercolour paints come in artists' or students' quality. Artists' quality paints flow better, mix better and look more vibrant on the paper. Students' quality paints may seem cheaper but you may end up using more paint, as they contain less pigment, so this may be a false economy.

Paints also come in pans or tubes. Pans are sold in compact sets, so they are good for painting outdoors, but tube colours are better if you are mixing large washes. I have used artists' quality tube colours for all the paintings in this book.

There is no need to buy a huge range of colours to start with, as you can usually mix what you need from the primary colours, plus a few extras.

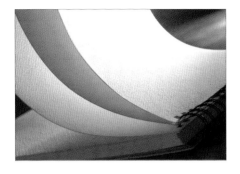

Paper

Watercolour paper comes in three different surfaces: Hot Pressed, which is smooth, Not, which has a slight texture, and Rough. It also comes in different weights. I have used 300gsm (140lb) Rough paper in this book, as it is heavy enough so that it does not usually cockle when washes are applied, and therefore does not need stretching before painting. The Rough surface is ideal for landscapes and is useful for many of the techniques I use, such as dry brush work.

Brushes

The **19mm (¾in) flat brush** is used to apply a wash when painting water, and to create a straight line for the horizon.

I used the **clear acrylic resin handl**e of a 13mm (½in) flat brush to scrape out rock shapes from drying paint.

I use a **large mop brush** for applying large washes, since this brush holds lots of paint.

A **hog fan brush** is a good stiff brush for creating textural effects, and the shape makes it ideal for flicking up grasses.

A no. 8 flat hog brush is also a stiff brush, and it is used for stippling on foliage.

A **no. 16 round brush** holds lots of paint and is good for applying fairly large washes.

A **no. 12 round brush** is also suitable for washes. It comes to a fine point, so is very versatile.

A **no. 8 round brush** holds a fair amount of paint and can be used for all but the finest details.

A **10mm (³/₈in) one-stroke sable brush** is useful for stippling on texture.

A **no. 4 round brush** is good for painting small details.

A **rigger** has long hair that comes to a very fine point, and was invented for painting the rigging on ships. It can be used to paint the finest details.

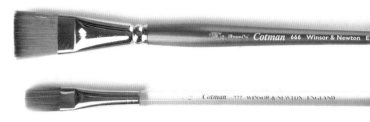

Top: a 19mm (¾in) flat brush and (bottom) a 13mm (½in) flat brush with a clear acrylic resin handle.

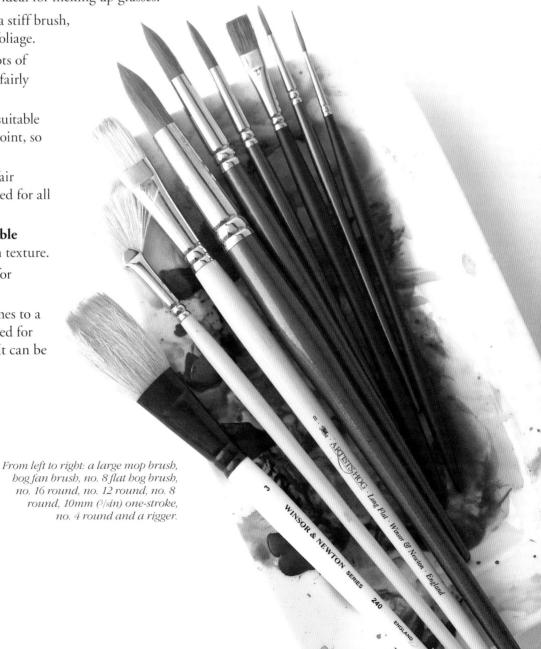

From left to right: a large mop brush, hog fan brush, no. 8 flat hog brush, no. 16 round, no. 12 round, no. 8 round, 10mm (³/₈in) one-stroke, no. 4 round and a rigger.

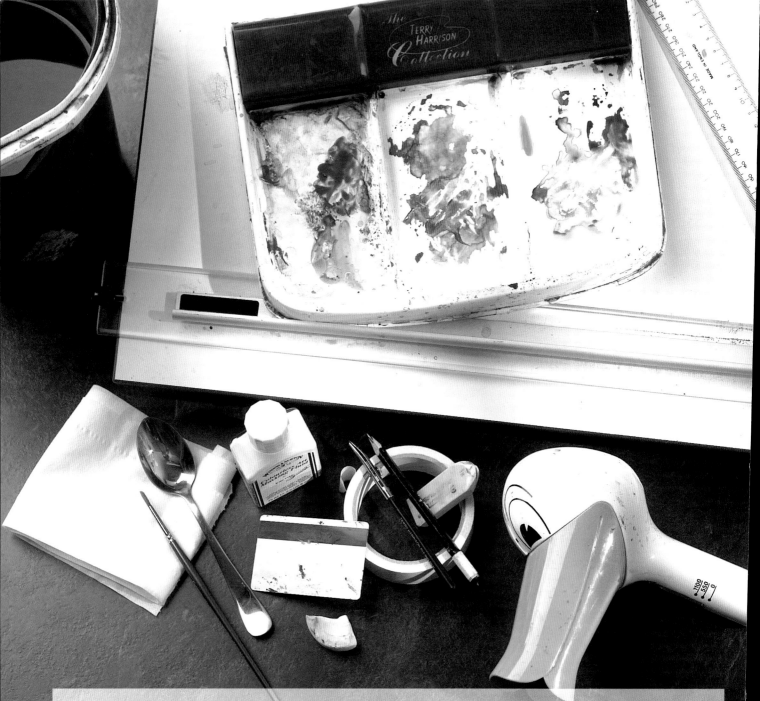

Other materials

I attach my watercolour paper to a **drawing board** using **masking tape**.

A **palette** is used for laying out your tube colours ready for painting. There are mixing wells for mixing washes.

A **ruler** can be used to help you paint straight lines.

A **plastic card** is used to scrape out colour to create a rocky texture.

Scrap paper torn from a magazine is useful for creating a paper mask.

Masking fluid is used with a **ruling pen** or **brush** to mask out details that you want to keep white. **Soap** is used to protect your brush: wet the brush and coat it in soap before using masking fluid. The fluid will wash out easily with the soap when you wash the brush after use.

A 4B or 2B **pencil** and **eraser** are used for transferring the image from the tracing on to watercolour paper. The handle of a **spoon** can be used to help transfer the image (see page 9).

I use a **bucket** instead of a water pot to wash out my brushes during painting, because the more water you use, the cleaner your brushes will be.

A **hairdryer** can be used to speed up the drying process.

Kitchen paper is useful for mopping up spills and to lift out colour while washes are wet.

Transferring the image

Tracings are provided at the front of this book for all the demonstration paintings and for the painting on pages 4–5. Follow the steps shown below to transfer the images on to watercolour paper. You can reuse each tracing several times to produce quite different paintings.

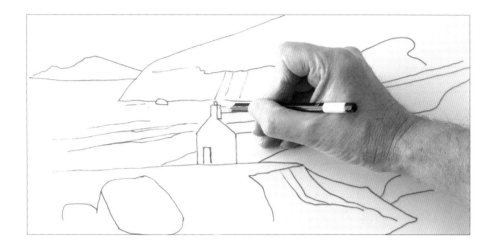

1 Place the tracing face down. Go over the lines on the back using a 4B or 2B pencil. You will be able to reuse this tracing several times without going over the pencil lines again.

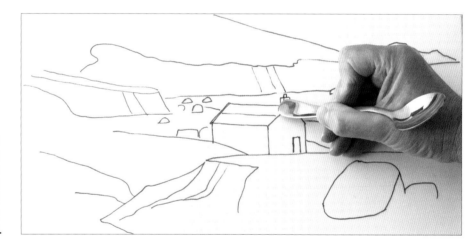

2 Tape a sheet of A3 watercolour paper down on a board and place the tracing, face up on top. Tape down the top of the tracing only. Use the end of spoon, a burnisher or a ballpoint pen lid to go over the lines.

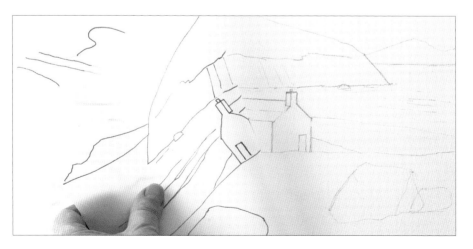

3 As you work, lift up the tracing from the bottom to see how the transfer of the image is going.

Mount Croagh Patrick

This is a fabulous view of Mount Croagh Patrick, a mountain near the town of Westport in County Mayo. This mountain is an important Catholic pilgrimage destination and the summit has a small chapel where mass is held each day. My painting includes some buildings on the water's edge which help to establish the scale of the distant peak. The flowers in the foreground add colour and interest to this peaceful scene.

TRACING 2

You will need

300gsm (140lb) Rough watercolour paper

Colours: raw sienna, French ultramarine, ultramarine violet, cobalt blue, burnt sienna, Hooker's green, burnt umber, green gold, cadmium yellow, permanent rose

Brushes: Large mop, no. 16 round, no. 8 flat hog, 19mm (¾in) flat, no. 8 round, rigger, hog fan, no. 4 round

Masking fluid, ruling pen and brush

Scrap paper from a magazine

To protect your good brushes from masking fluid, rub the damp brush into ordinary household soap before dipping it in the masking fluid. As soon as you have finished using it, wash the brush and the masking fluid will come out with the soap.

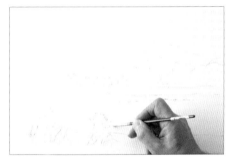

1 Transfer the image on to watercolour paper. Mask the reeds and grasses in the foreground with a ruling pen and masking fluid, then use a no. 4 brush to mask the flowers, the ripples on the water and the buildings.

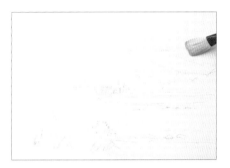

2 Wet the sky area with the large mop brush and clean water, going round the mountains. Paint in raw sienna at the bottom of the sky.

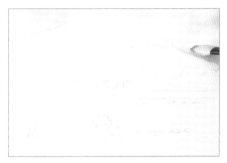

3 While the first wash is wet, paint in ultramarine, leaving gaps for clouds.

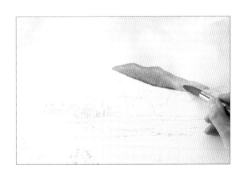

4 Use the no. 16 round brush to paint the distant hills with a mix of ultramarine violet and a touch of cobalt blue.

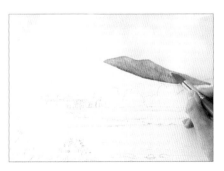

5 Drop in raw sienna wet into wet. This will create an interesting textural effect as the raw sienna pushes away the other colours.

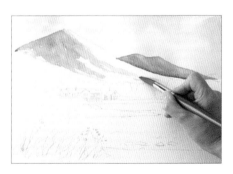

6 Paint cobalt blue on the left-hand mountain, leaving gaps and extending the wash out to the right. Allow to dry.

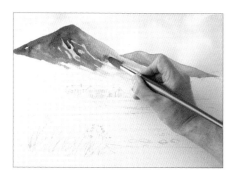

7 Paint a mix of ultramarine violet and burnt sienna on to the darker part of the left-hand mountain.

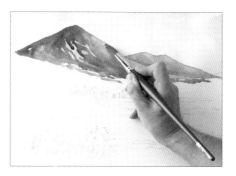

8 While the purple wash is wet, drop in raw sienna, which will create a textured look and create the sunlit areas of the mountain.

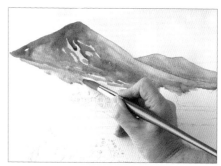

9 Paint a mix of raw sienna and burnt sienna to paint the area just below the mountain.

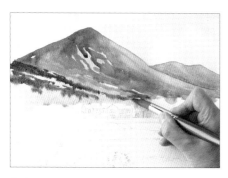

10 While this wash is wet, drop in ultamarine violet and burnt sienna, to create texture. Allow to dry.

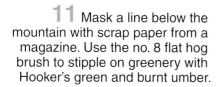

11 Mask a line below the mountain with scrap paper from a magazine. Use the no. 8 flat hog brush to stipple on greenery with Hooker's green and burnt umber.

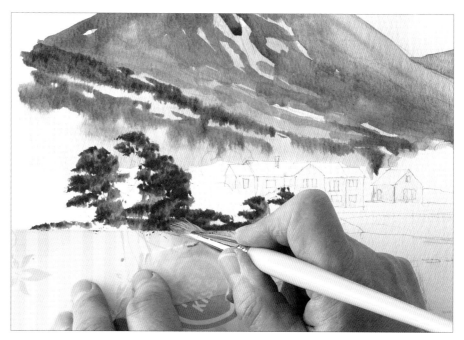

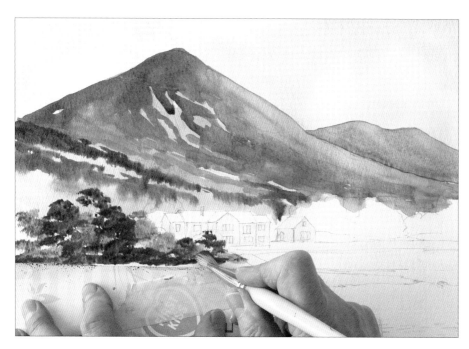

12 Stipple on green gold and burnt sienna to vary the greens.

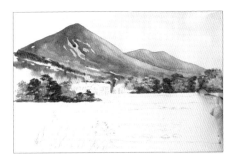

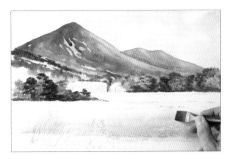

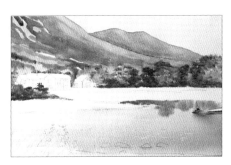

13 Continue stippling on greenery on the right-hand side of the painting with Hooker's green and burnt umber, and green gold and burnt sienna.

14 Change to the 19mm (¾in) flat brush and wet the water area, then paint on a wash of ultramarine, beginning in the foreground and going up. As the paint mixes with the water, it gets lighter higher up.

15 Use the no. 8 flat hog brush and add a touch of ultramarine to the Hooker's green and burnt umber mix to drop in reflections of the trees wet into wet.

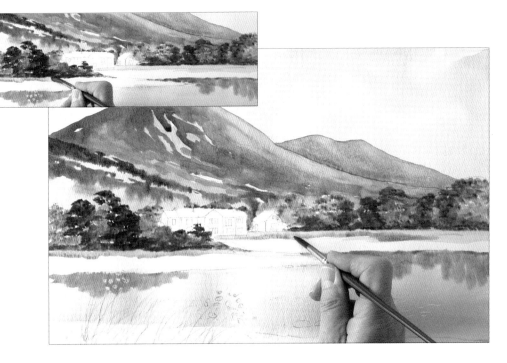

16 Paint the fields with the no. 8 round brush and green gold. Tone down the brightness of the green by dropping in Hooker's green and burnt sienna wet into wet.

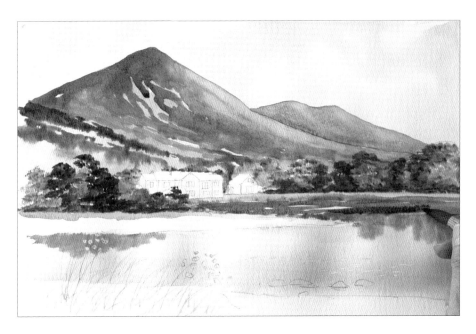

17 Paint the dark tones at the water's edge with the no. 16 brush and ultramarine with burnt umber.

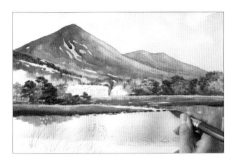

18 Paint some rocks at the water's edge in the same way.

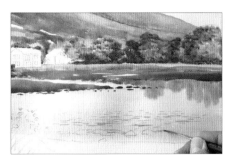

19 Use the rigger brush to paint ripples in the foreground water with ultramarine.

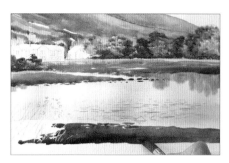

20 Paint the foreshore with the no. 16 brush and ultramarine and burnt umber.

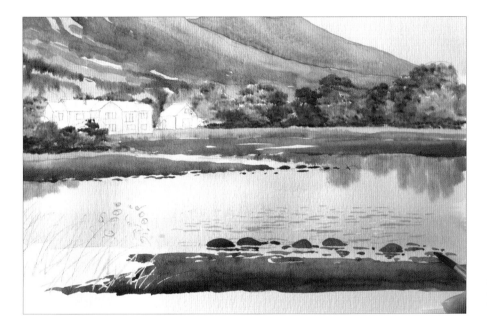

21 Use the no. 8 round brush and the same mix to paint rocks.

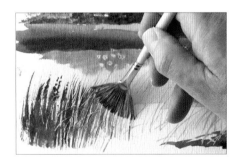

22 Change to the hog fan brush and use a mix of Hooker's green, burnt umber and ultramarine to flick up grasses in the foreground.

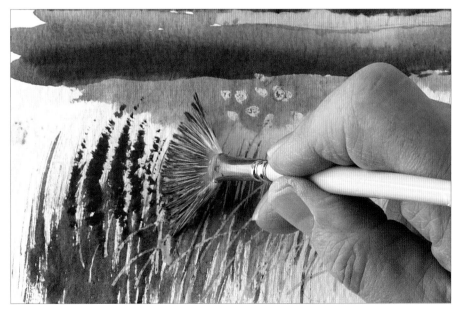

23 Use the tips of the hog bristles to create seed heads.

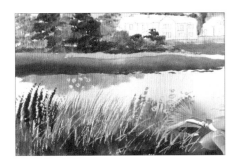

24 Stipple on more seed heads with green gold. Allow to dry.

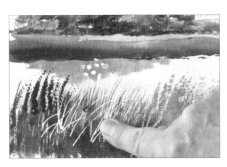

25 Remove the masking fluid by rubbing with clean fingers.

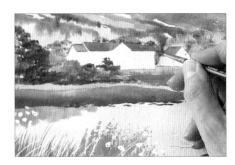

26 Paint the roofs of the buildings with the no. 4 brush and ultramarine with burnt umber.

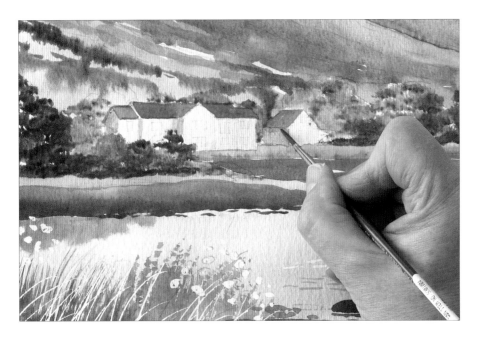

27 Paint the buildings with a very pale mix of raw sienna and burnt sienna. Leave them to dry. Add shadows mixed from ultramarine violet and burnt sienna.

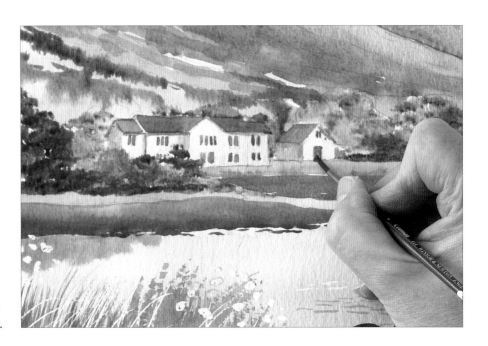

28 Paint in the windows and doors with a mix of ultramarine and burnt umber.

14

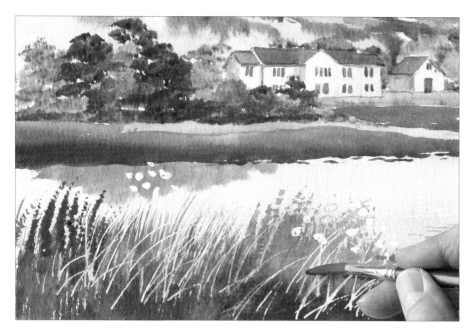

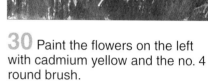

30 Paint the flowers on the left with cadmium yellow and the no. 4 round brush.

29 Paint a light wash of green gold over the masked grasses with the no. 8 round.

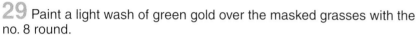

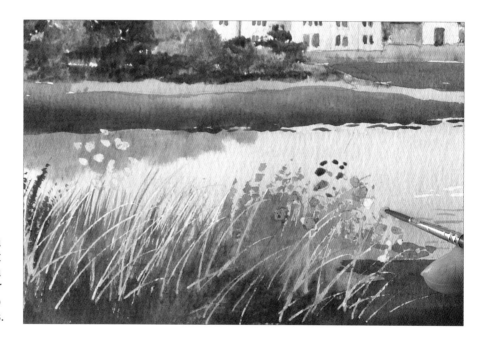

31 Use the same brush and a wash of permanent rose to paint the flowers on the right. Drop in a stronger mix of the same colour while the first wash is still wet, to vary the tones.

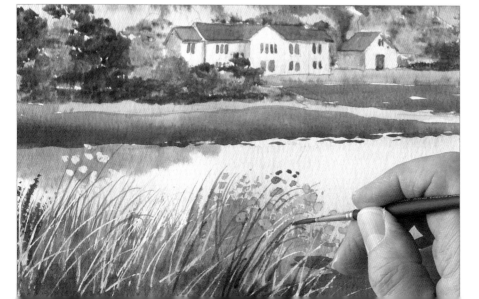

32 Change to the rigger brush and Hooker's green with burnt umber to paint dark grasses in the foreground.

Overleaf

The finished painting.

15

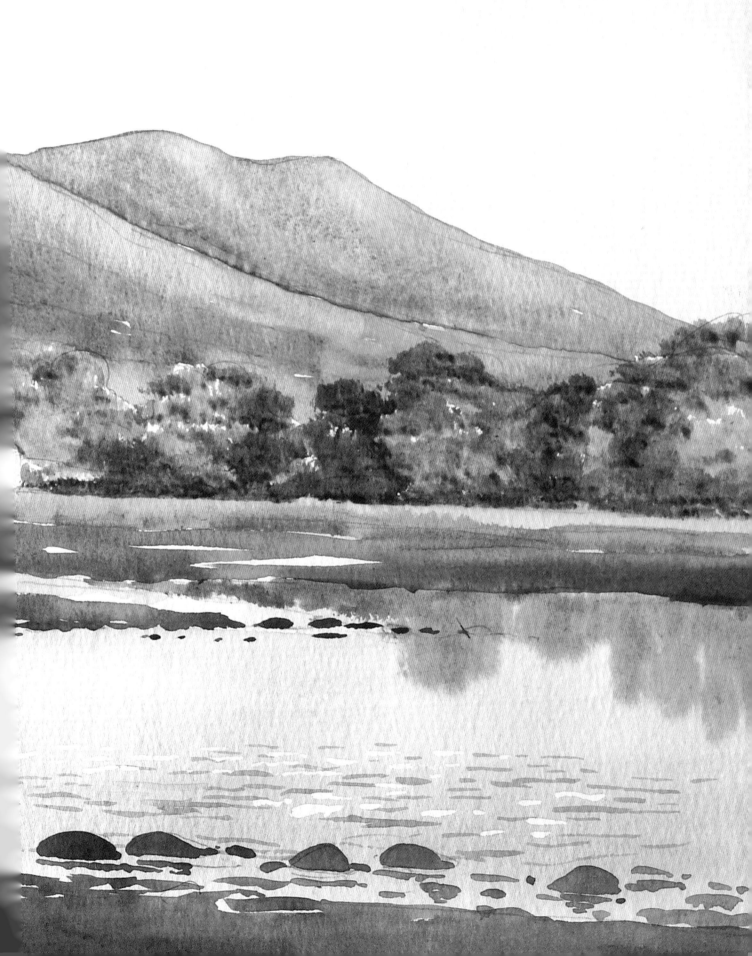

Dunguaire Castle

Dunguaire Castle must be the most photographed castle in Ireland. This 16th century tower house is situated on the south-east shore of Galway Bay near Kinvara. I have used the tower as a focal point which is just off-centre in the painting. The castle is surrounded on three sides by water, which is a great excuse to use reflections in the foreground.

TRACING

3

Tip

To scrape out the rocks on the moat shoreline, use either the clear acrylic resin handle of your paintbrush, or the corner of a plastic card.

You will need

300gsm (140lb) Rough watercolour paper

Colours: raw sienna, ultramarine, burnt umber, Hooker's green, cobalt blue, green gold, olive green, burnt sienna, permanent rose

Brushes: large mop, no. 8 round, no. 16 round, 10mm (³⁄₈in) one-stroke, rigger, 13mm (½in) flat with clear acrylic resin handle, no. 4 round

Masking fluid

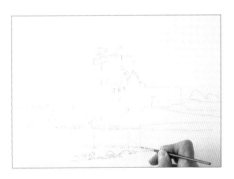

1 Transfer the scene on to watercolour paper. Mask the ripples in the water with masking fluid and a no 4. brush.

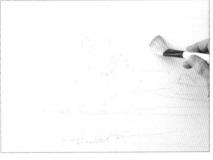

2 Wet the sky area with the large mop brush. Drop in raw sienna.

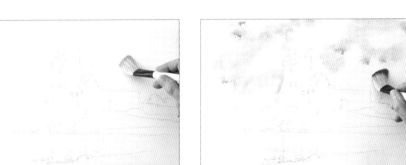

3 Paint the blue of the sky with ultramarine, leaving spaces for clouds.

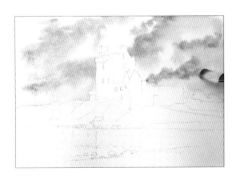

4 Still working wet into wet, drop in the darker parts of the clouds with a mix of burnt umber and ultramarine. Allow to dry.

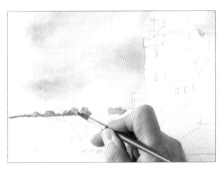

5 Paint the trees in the background with the no. 8 round and a mix of Hooker's green and cobalt blue. While this is wet, drop in green gold.

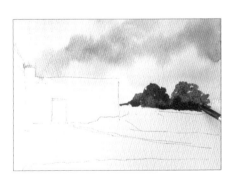

6 Paint the trees on the right with a mix of olive green and ultramarine.

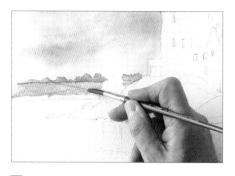

7 Paint below the trees with olive green and raw sienna.

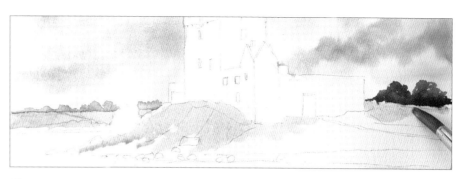

8 Use the no. 16 round to paint the hillock with olive green and raw sienna. Continue painting the fields on the right.

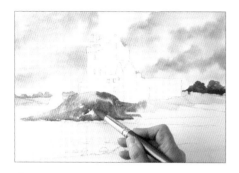

9 While the wash is still wet, drop in a mix of olive green and burnt umber.

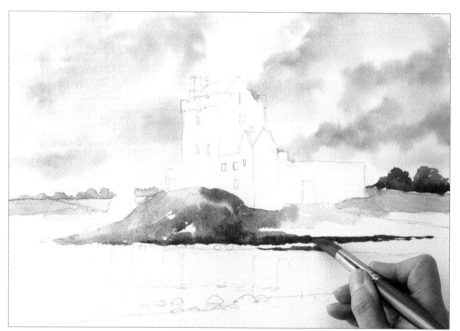

10 Still working wet into wet, mix Hooker's green and burnt umber and run this along the base of the hillock.

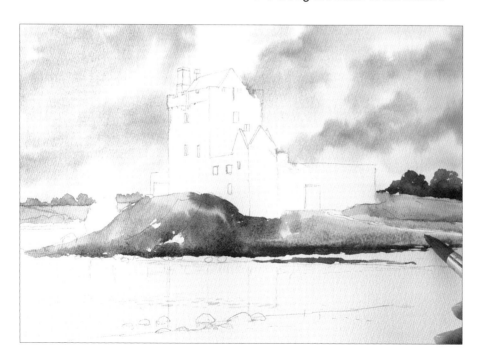

11 Paint grass on the hillock with olive green.

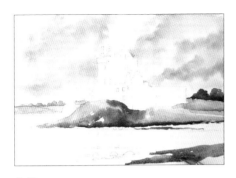

12 Paint the foreground with olive green and drop in burnt umber wet into wet.

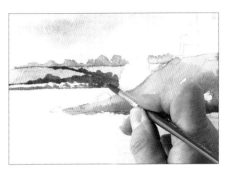

13 Use the no. 8 round to paint hedgerows in the background with olive green and ultramarine.

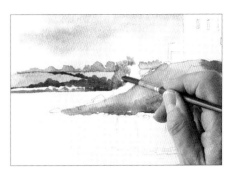

14 Paint the distant bush with green gold.

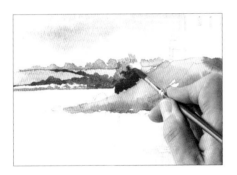

15 Paint the right-hand side of the bush with a darker mix of Hooker's green and burnt umber. Allow to dry.

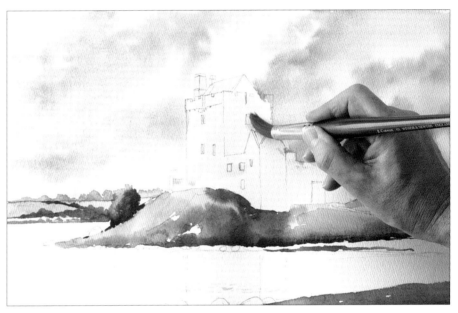

16 Change to the no. 16 brush and paint a pale wash of raw sienna and burnt sienna over the castle.

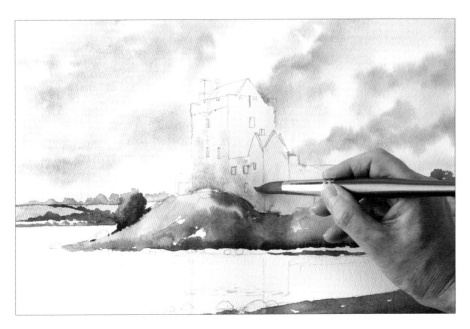

17 While this wash is wet, drop in a mix of cobalt blue and burnt sienna to create texture.

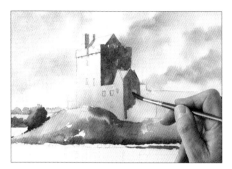

18 Change to the no. 8 brush and paint the shaded parts of the castle with ultramarine, burnt sienna and permanent rose.

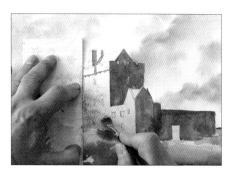

19 Pick up the same shadow mix with the 10mm (³⁄₈in) one-stroke brush. Place a paper mask with a straight edge over the sky area and stipple texture on to the castle.

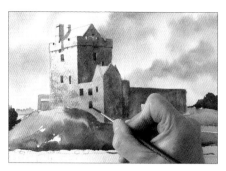

20 Paint the details of the castle with the rigger brush and a mix of ultramarine and burnt umber.

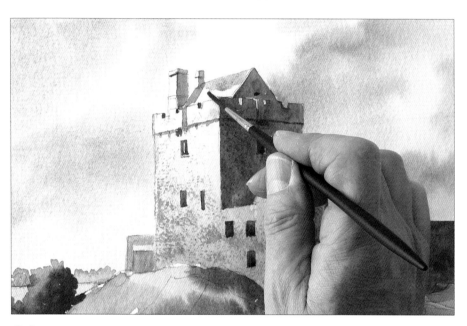

21 Darken the side of the sloping roof with a mix of cobalt blue and raw sienna.

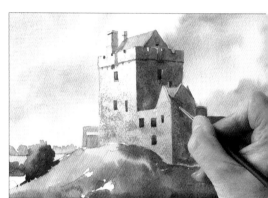

22 Use the same mix to paint other shaded details.

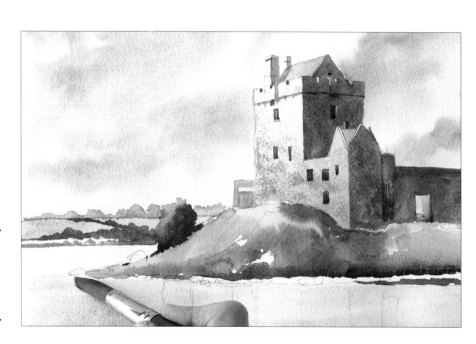

23 Wet the water area with a no. 16 brush and clean water. Then paint a wash of ultramarine, starting at the bottom, with horizontal strokes. As you go further up, the water will dilute the wash and the colour will be paler.

21

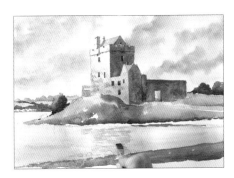

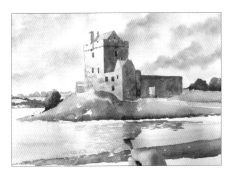

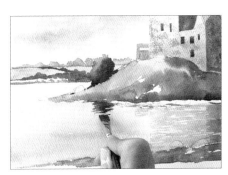

24 Mix raw sienna and cobalt blue and use the 10mm (³/₈in) one-stroke brush to paint the reflection of the castle with horizontal strokes.

25 Make a darker mix of the same colours and paint the reflection of the shaded part of the castle in the same way.

26 Mix olive green and ultramarine and paint the reflection of the bush.

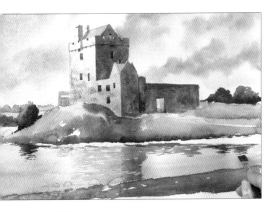

27 Paint reflections of the darker greens with Hooker's green.

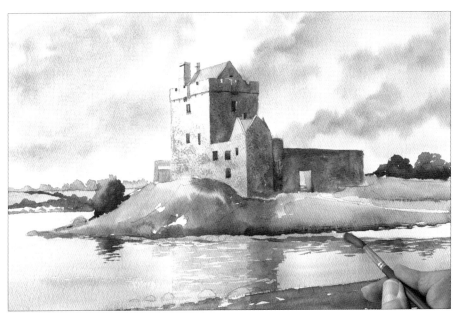

28 Use the no. 8 brush to paint a wash of raw sienna around the waterline.

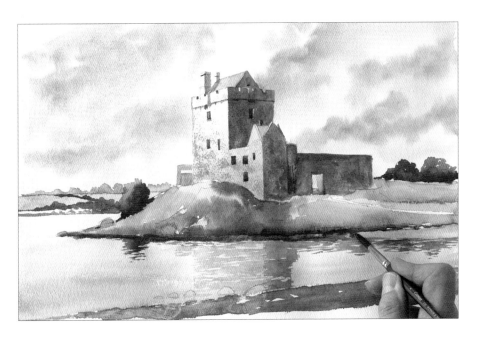

29 While the raw sienna wash is wet, drop in ultramarine and burnt umber on top.

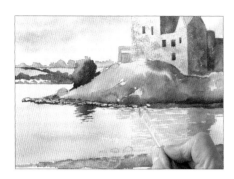

30 Use the end of the clear acrylic resin brush handle to scrape out rock shapes around the waterline.

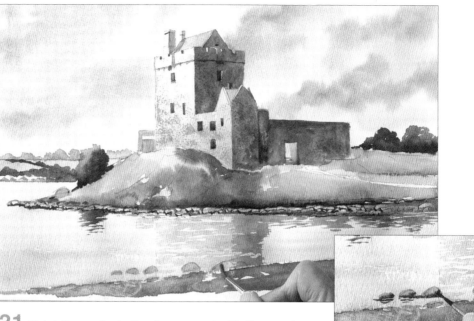

31 Paint the rocks in the foreground with the no. 4 round brush and raw sienna.

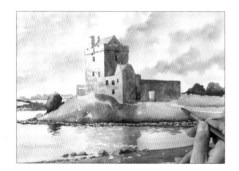

32 Use a no. 8 brush to paint raw sienna on the path leading to the castle.

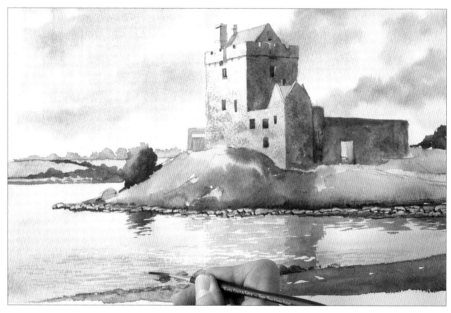

33 Rub off the masking fluid with a clean finger. Paint ripples on the foreground water with the rigger and ultramarine.

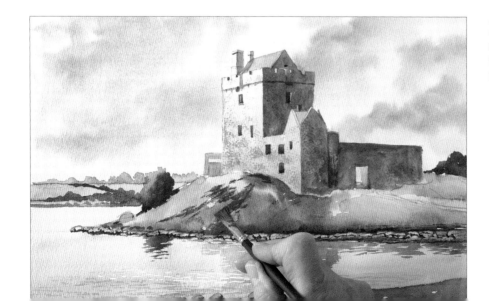

34 Use the 10mm (³⁄₈in) one-stroke brush to paint detail on the hillock with a dry mix of burnt umber and olive green.

Overleaf

The finished painting.

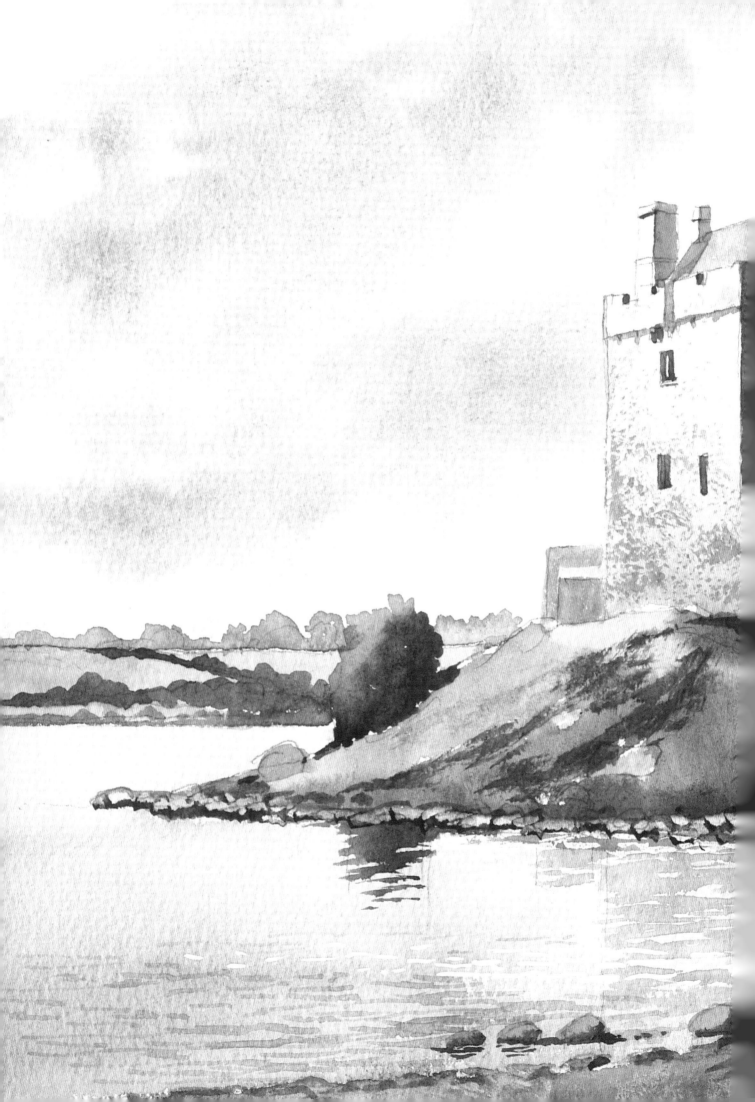

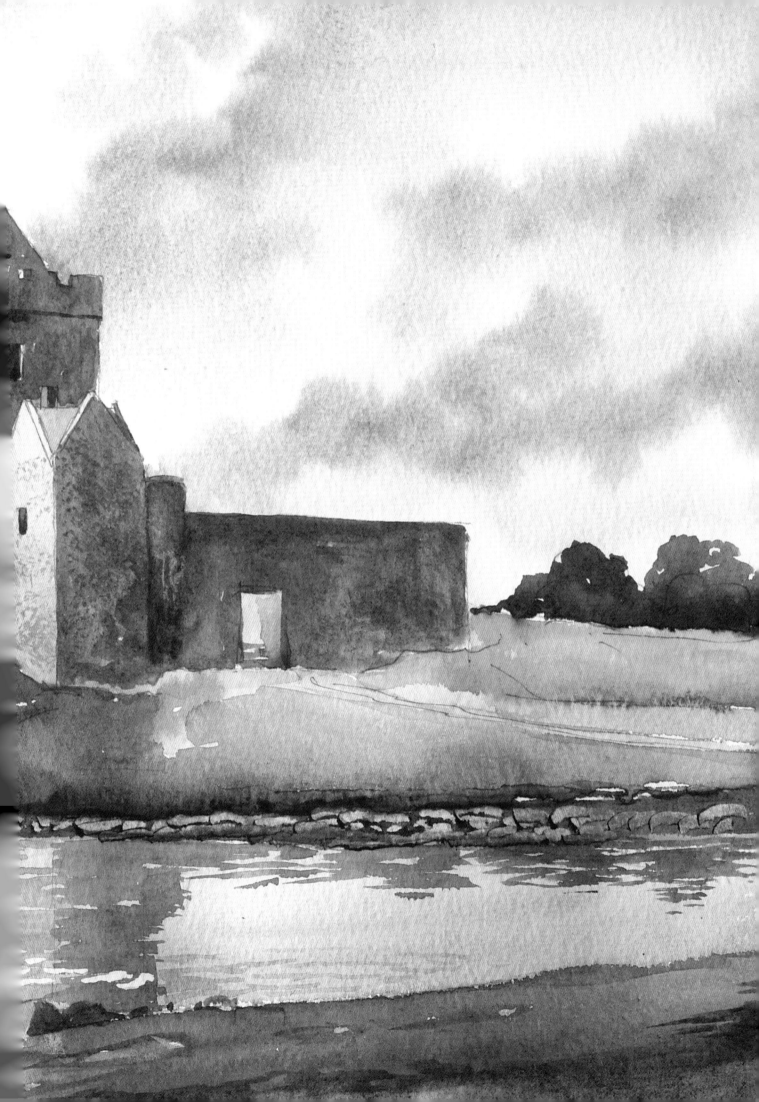

Keem Bay

Keem Bay is to the west of Achill Island in County Mayo, the largest island in Ireland. The old cottage sheltered in the bay makes a stunning subject to paint. The temptation is to change the tin roof for a traditional thatched roof, but maybe that would be a project for the future. You will need a plastic card to create the cliffs on the headland and the rocks in the foreground. I know this technique is tricky to achieve straight away, so I suggest you have a little practice first.

Another way to create texture on the rocks and cliffs is to use the dry brush technique.

TRACING

4

You will need

300gsm (140lb) Rough watercolour paper

Colours: raw sienna, French ultramarine, permanent rose, burnt sienna, burnt umber, cobalt blue, green gold, olive green, permanent sap green, Hooker's green

Brushes: no. 4 round, no. 16 round, no. 8 round, 10mm (3/8in) one-stroke, hog fan brush

Masking fluid

Plastic card

1 Transfer the scene on to watercolour paper. Mask the shoreline under the cliffs and the crests of the waves using a no. 4 brush and masking fluid. Wet the sky area and paint raw sienna in the lower part of the sky with the no. 16 brush.

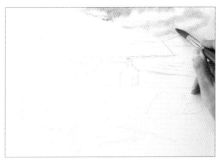

2 While the raw sienna wash is wet, drop in ultramarine, leaving spaces for cloud shapes. Allow to dry.

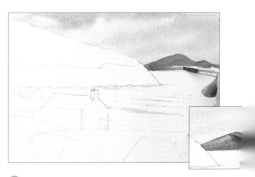

3 Mix ultramarine, permanent rose and a touch of burnt sienna to paint the distant headland with the no. 8 brush. While this is wet, drop in raw sienna to suggest sunlit areas.

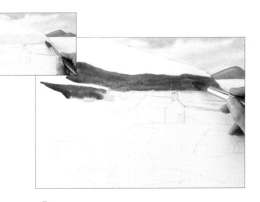

4 Use the no. 16 brush to paint the cliff face with a thick mix of raw sienna. While this is wet, paint thick burnt umber and ultramarine over the top.

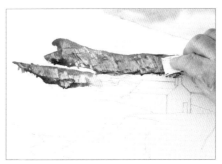

5 Use the edge of a plastic card to scrape out colour, creating the rocky texture of the cliffs.

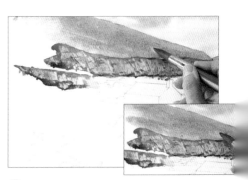

6 Paint the top of the headland with the no. 16 brush and cobalt blue and burnt sienna. Drop in green gold wet into wet.

26

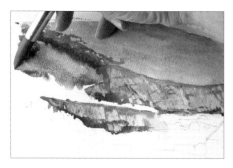

7 Paint the grassy area coming forwards with olive green, then drop in a darker green mixed from olive green and raw sienna.

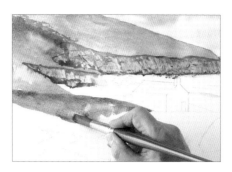

8 Paint a mix of permanent sap green and burnt sienna coming forwards towards the cottage.

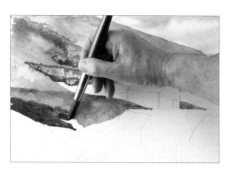

9 Further forwards, darken the area with a mix of permanent sap green and burnt umber. Allow to dry.

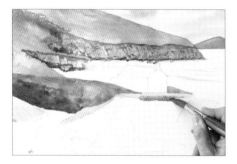

10 Paint the top edge of the greener area further forwards with raw sienna and green gold, then drop in olive green wet into wet.

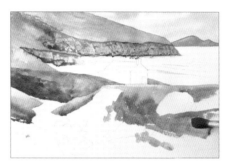

11 Continue painting the grassy area with a mix of olive green and burnt umber.

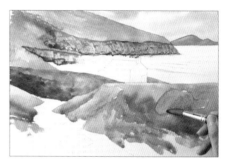

12 Mix a grey from cobalt blue and burnt sienna and wash this over the white areas to create rocks.

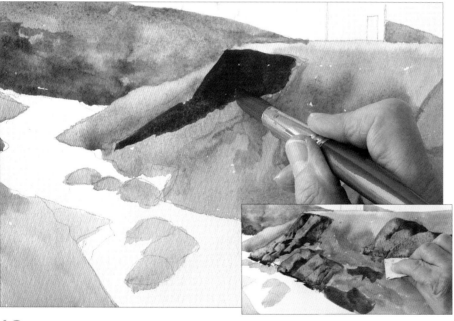

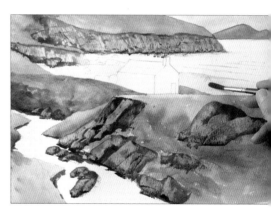

14 Paint the sand on the beach with a wash of raw sienna. Allow to dry.

13 Paint the rocks in the stream with the same mix. Then paint a thick mix of burnt umber and ultramarine over the lighter rock colour. Before this dries, scrape out rock texture with a plastic card.

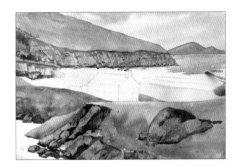

15 Change to the 10mm (³⁄₈in) one-stroke brush and paint the sea with horizontal strokes in ultramarine. Add a touch of permanent sap green to the mix coming further forwards.

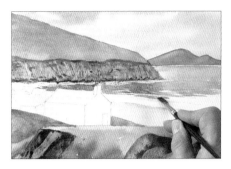

16 Bring the horizontal strokes forwards, going over the masked area and leaving some white paper as well.

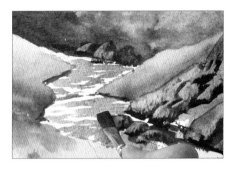

17 Paint the stream with the same brush and ultramarine, leaving white for ripples. Allow to dry.

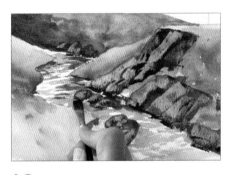

18 Paint darker brush strokes in the water with a mix of ultramarine and burnt umber.

19 Use the no. 8 brush to paint details of the cliffs and rocks with a dark mix of ultramarine and burnt umber.

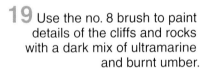

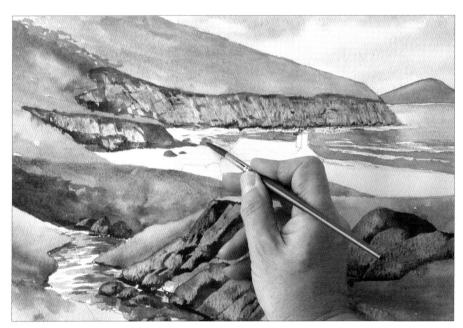

20 Paint the lighter side of the cottage with a pale mix of raw sienna and cobalt blue. While this is wet, drop in cobalt blue at the bottom of the wall and let it bleed upwards to create an uneven wash. Allow to dry.

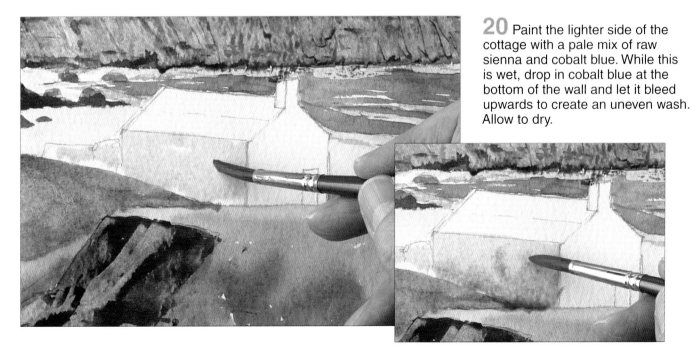

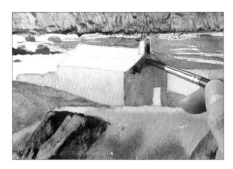

21 Mix cobalt blue and burnt sienna and use the no. 8 brush to paint the shaded end of the cottage. While this is still wet, drop in a darker mix of the same colours at the top and let it bleed down.

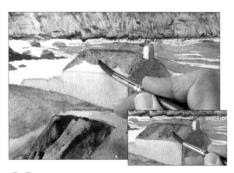

22 Paint the left-hand side of the roof with burnt sienna. While this is wet, touch in cobalt blue.

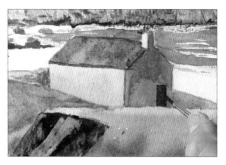

23 Use the no. 4 round and ultramarine with burnt umber to paint the darks of the doorway and the roof details.

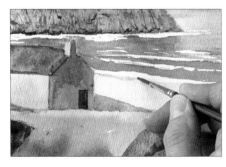

24 Remove the masking fluid with a clean finger. Use the no. 4 brush to paint shade under the surf with a pale wash of cobalt blue.

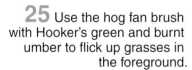

25 Use the hog fan brush with Hooker's green and burnt umber to flick up grasses in the foreground.

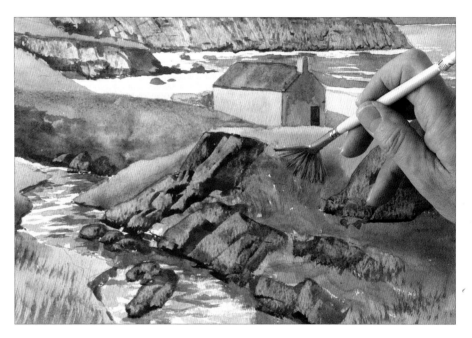

26 Use the no. 4 brush and a mix of ultramarine and burnt umber to paint texture on the side of the cottage.

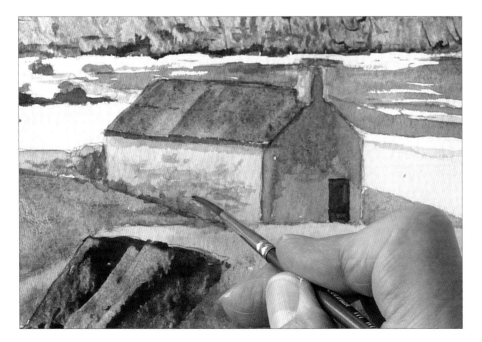

Overleaf

The finished painting.

29

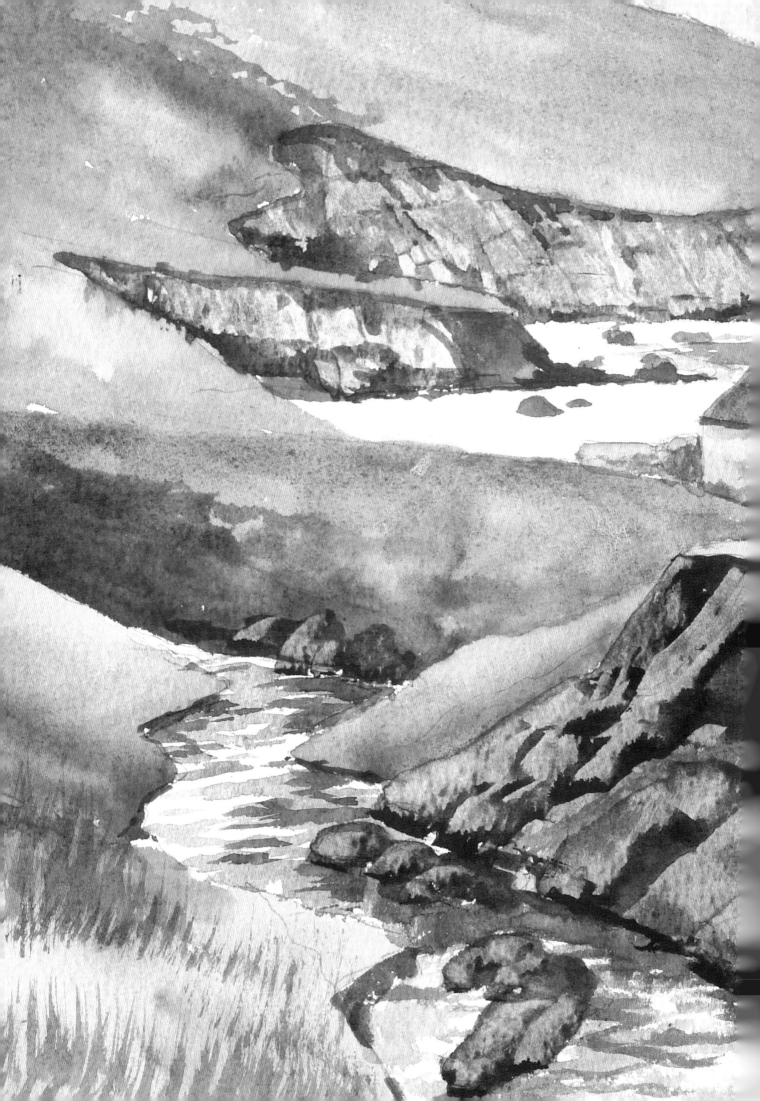

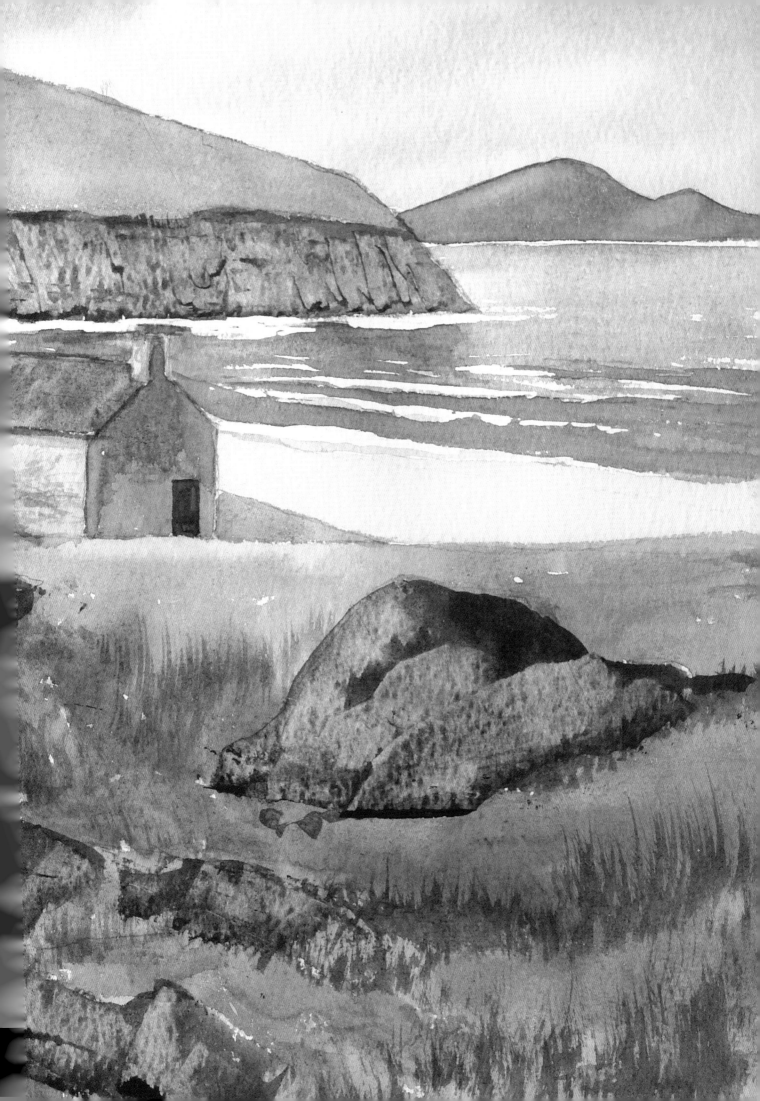

The Cliffs of Moher

These cliffs are located near Doolin in County Clare on the west coast, and are one of Ireland's top visitor attractions. The cliffs are 214m (702 ft) high at the highest point and extend for 8km (5 miles) along the Atlantic coast. The view I have chosen for this project is a fairly simple composition: the cliffs stretch out along the coast, gradually reducing in size and becoming lighter and bluer in colour, giving the impression of distance. The grasses and flowers on the clifftop add some colour and interest to the foreground.

You will need

300gsm (140lb) Rough watercolour paper

Colours: raw sienna, French ultramarine, burnt umber, cobalt blue, burnt sienna, olive green, permanent sap green, green gold, permanent rose

Brushes: no. 4 round, large mop, 10mm (³/₈in) one-stroke, no. 16 round, no. 8 round, 19mm (¾in) flat, hog fan brush, rigger

Masking fluid and ruling pen

Plastic card

Ruler

Tip

To achieve the best results when painting cliffs, use Rough paper, don't have the paint too wet, and scrape the paint off with what is best described as a short, sharp, downward motion of the plastic card.

TRACING

5

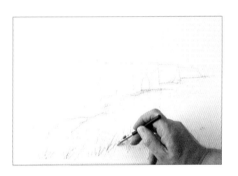

1 Transfer the scene on to watercolour paper. Mask off the surf at the base of the cliffs with masking fluid and the no. 4 brush. Use a ruling pen to mask the grasses in the foreground.

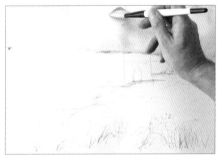

2 Wet the sky with a large mop brush and clean water. Paint on a thin wash of raw sienna. While this is wet, drop in ultramarine, leaving spaces for cloud shapes.

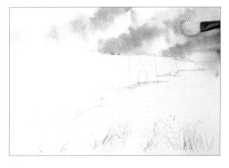

3 Mix ultramarine and burnt umber and paint the darker parts of the clouds wet into wet. Allow to dry.

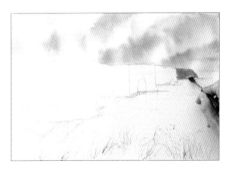

4 Paint the most distant cliffs with the 10mm (³/₈in) one-stroke brush and a mix of cobalt blue with a touch of burnt sienna.

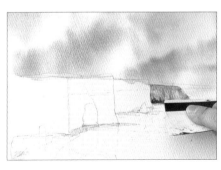

5 While the paint is still wet, use a plastic card to scrape out texture.

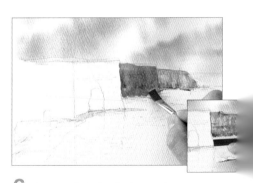

6 Use a slightly darker mix of the same colours to paint the next section of cliff coming forwards. Scrape out with a plastic card as before.

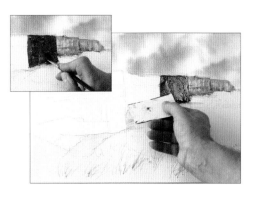

7 Further forwards, continue painting with a slightly darker, browner mix of the same colours, and scrape out again.

8 Paint the next section with a thick mix of raw sienna.

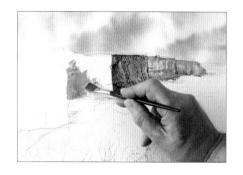

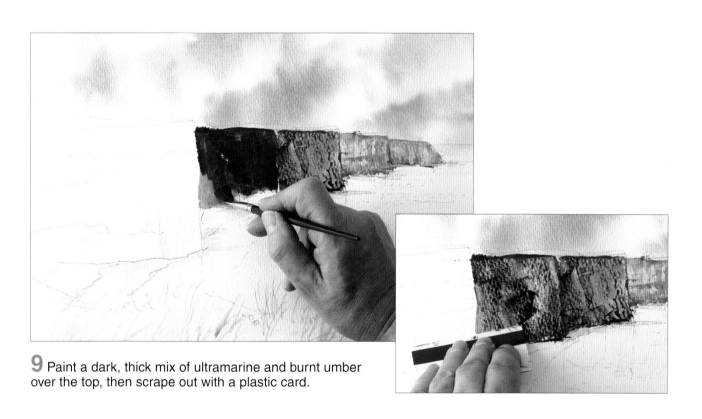

9 Paint a dark, thick mix of ultramarine and burnt umber over the top, then scrape out with a plastic card.

10 Use the no. 16 brush to paint raw sienna on the nearest cliffs, then add a dark mix of burnt sienna and cobalt blue. Mix the two colours on the page, then scrape out the area with a plastic card.

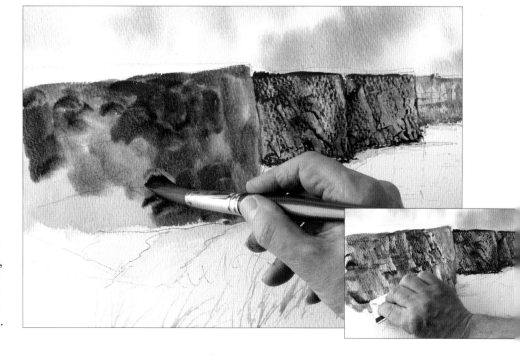

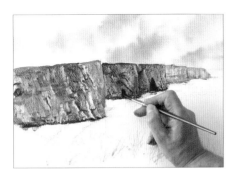

11 Paint caves in the cliffs with the no. 8 round brush and a mix of ultramarine and burnt umber.

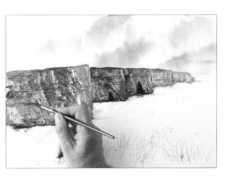

12 Paint in horizontal lines to suggest the different strata of rock in the cliff face.

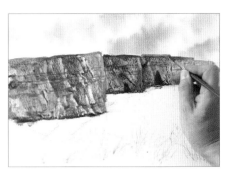

13 Paint the top of the distant cliffs with a mix of olive green and cobalt blue.

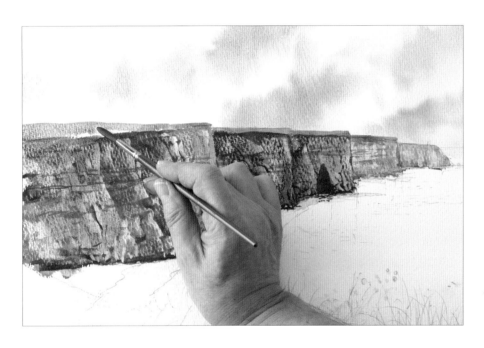

14 Paint the grass at the top of the nearer cliffs with olive green.

15 Wet the water area with clean water. Use the 19mm (¾in) flat brush and a pale mix of ultramarine to paint the water, starting with the horizon. Use a ruler to help you paint a straight line as shown.

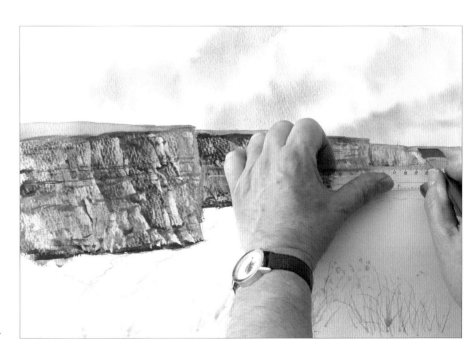

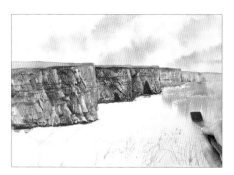

16 Add a touch of permanent sap green to the ultramarine and stroke the wash downwards.

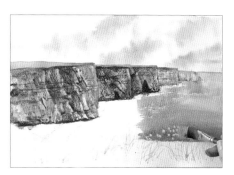

17 Paint the sea further forwards with horizontal strokes and strengthen the mix towards the foreground.

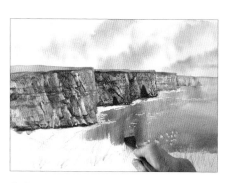

18 Make the mix stronger still as you paint up to the foreground cliff face.

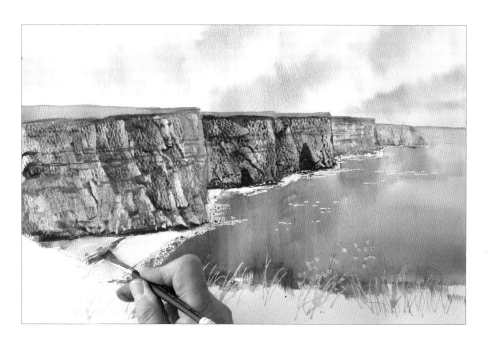

19 Using the same brush, paint the beach below the cliffs with a wash of raw sienna, then while this is wet, drop in burnt umber and ultramarine.

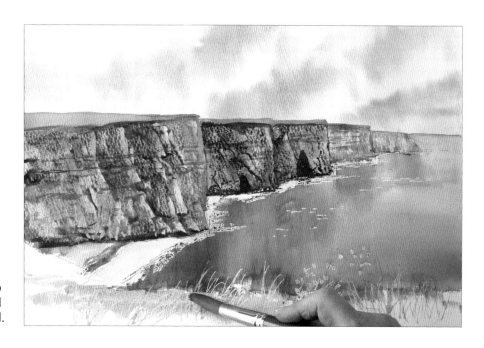

20 Paint the foreground clifftop with the no. 16 round brush and green gold.

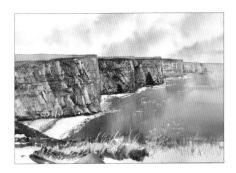

21 Mix a darker green from permanent sap green and burnt umber and paint this in wet into wet.

22 Use the hog fan brush and the same green to flick up grasses over the masked area. Allow to dry.

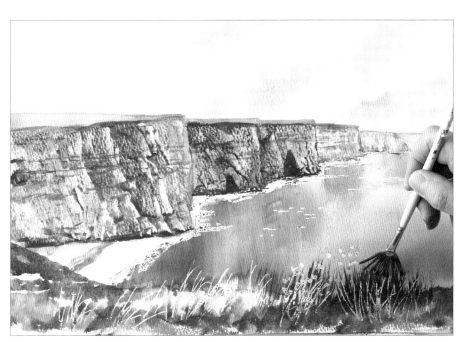

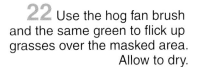

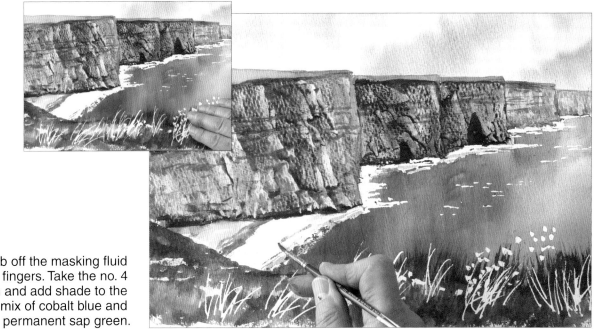

23 Rub off the masking fluid with clean fingers. Take the no. 4 round brush and add shade to the surf with a mix of cobalt blue and permanent sap green.

24 Paint some ripples on the sea with the same brush and colour.

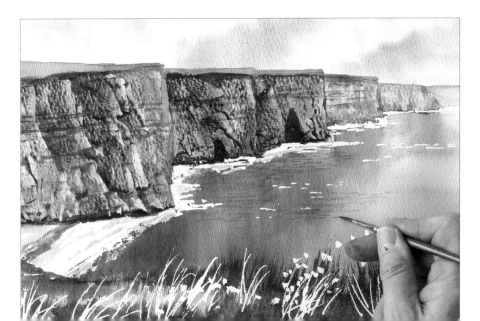

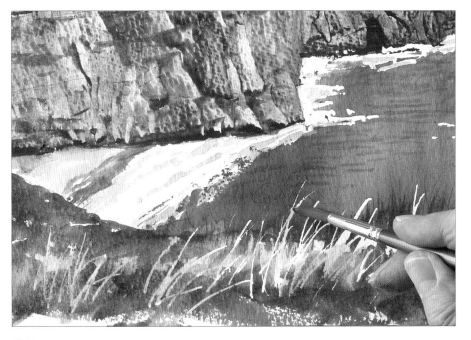

25 Use the no. 8 round to paint green gold over the foreground grasses.

26 Paint the flower heads with permanent rose.

27 Use the rigger to paint darker grasses among the flower heads with permanent sap green and burnt umber.

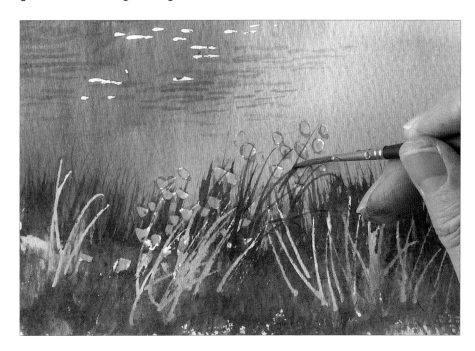

28 Stipple detail on the beach with the 10mm (³⁄₈in) one-stroke brush and burnt umber with ultramarine.

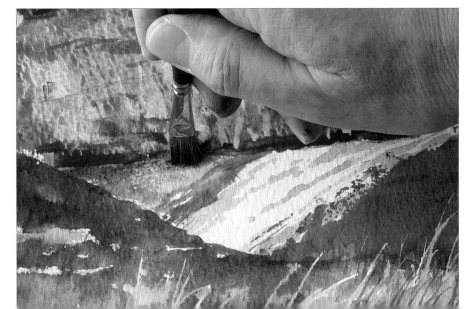

Overleaf

The finished painting.

37

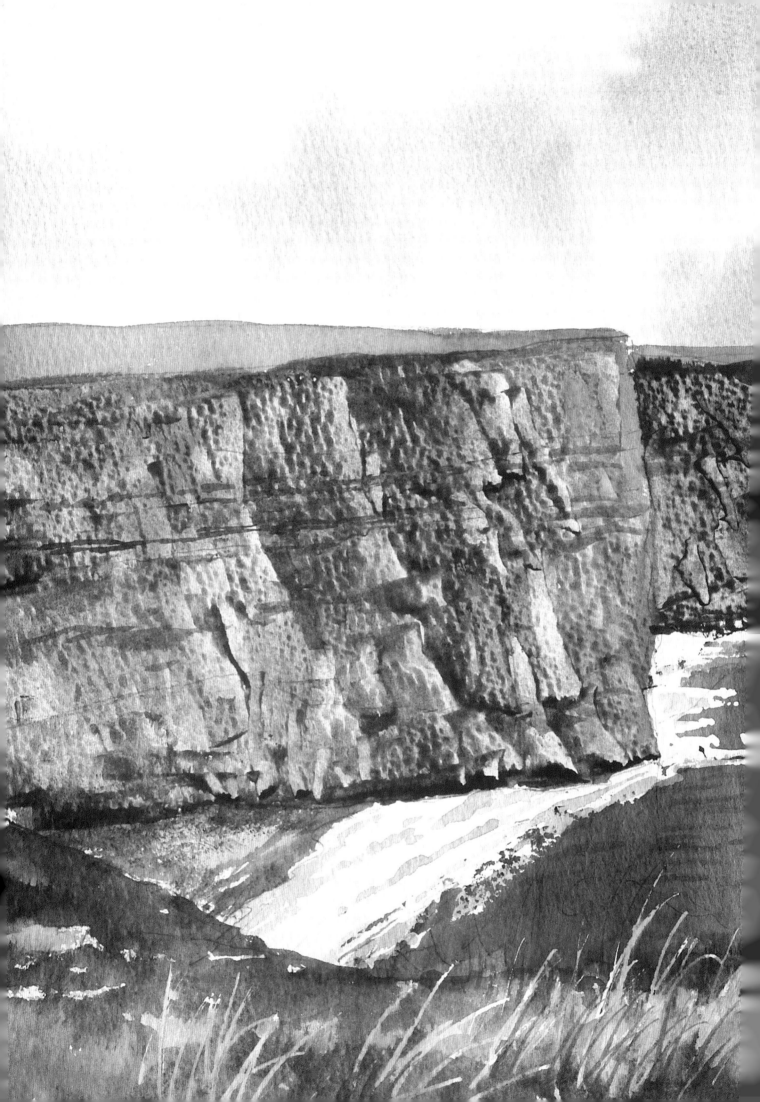

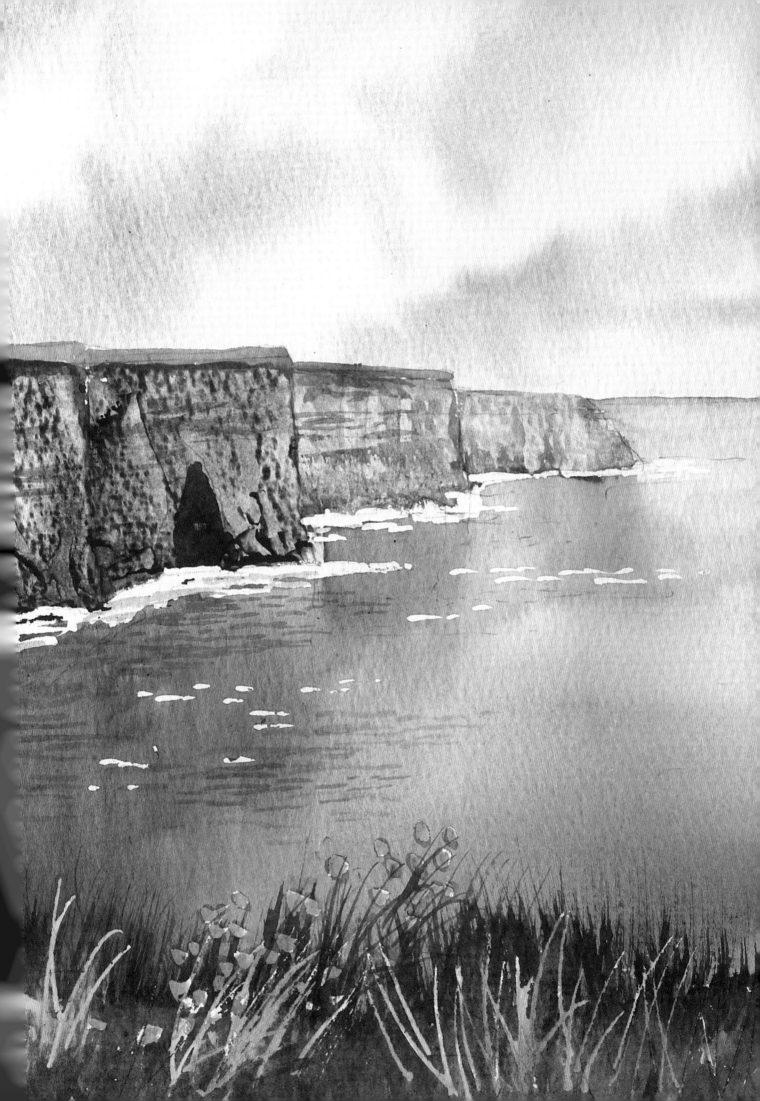

Dublin Doorway

In Dublin's fair city, where the doors are so pretty, many a true word is spoken in jest! But seriously, an outstanding feature of the Dublin streets is the many magnificent Georgian doorways. The doorway I have chosen for this project is not too complicated but it presents just enough of a challenge. When painting a subject such as this, you can get bogged down with too much detail, as many of the doorways are extremely ornate.

You will need

300gsm (140lb) Rough watercolour paper

Colours: raw sienna, cobalt blue, burnt sienna, French ultramarine, burnt umber, permanent rose, green gold, permanent sap green, olive green, Hooker's green, cadmium red

Brushes: no. 16 round, no. 12 round, no. 4 round, no. 8 round, rigger

Masking fluid and brush

Ruler

TRACING

6

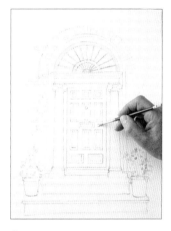

1 Transfer the scene on to watercolour paper and mask the window and door details and the flowers with masking fluid.

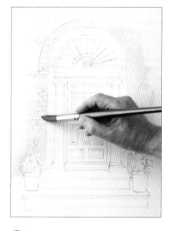

2 Use the no. 16 round to paint a wash of raw sienna over the walls.

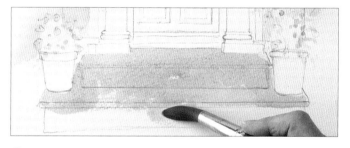

3 Mix a light grey from cobalt blue and burnt sienna and wash it over the steps.

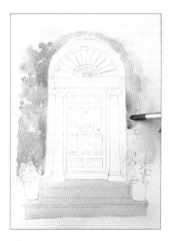

4 Wash burnt sienna over the brickwork, keeping it loose to create texture and leaving some of the first wash showing through.

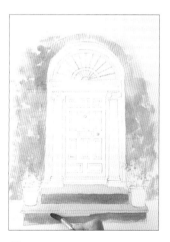

5 Use the no. 12 round and a mix of ultramarine and burnt umber to paint the shaded parts of the steps.

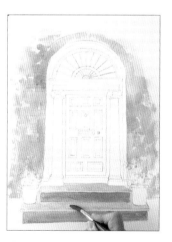

6 Use a lighter wash of the same colours to add tone on the flat parts of the steps. Leave a lighter line at the edge of each step.

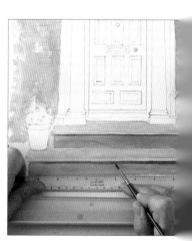

7 Use a no. 4 brush and a ruler to paint shadow under the edge of each step with the ultramarine and burnt umber mix.

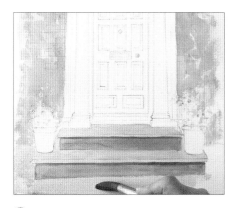

8 Paint a light wash on the pavement with the no. 16 brush and burnt sienna with cobalt blue.

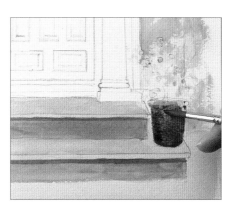

9 Paint the terracotta pots with the no. 8 round and burnt sienna. Drop in ultramarine and permanent rose on the left-hand side wet into wet.

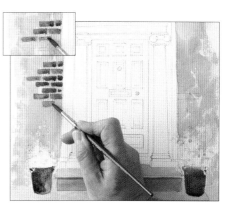

10 Paint in some bricks with burnt sienna, then change to burnt sienna with cobalt blue for variety.

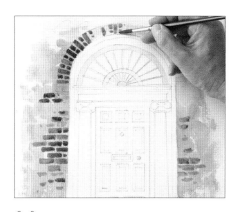

11 Paint a few individual bricks on the right of the door, then continue, painting bricks in a variety of shades around the semicircular window above the door.

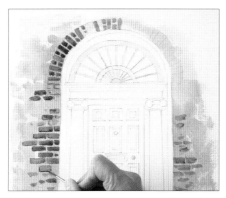

12 Use the rigger and a mix of burnt umber and ultramarine to paint shadow to the left and at the bottom of the bricks.

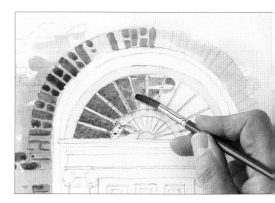

13 Paint over the masked details of the semicircular window with the no. 8 brush and ultramarine.

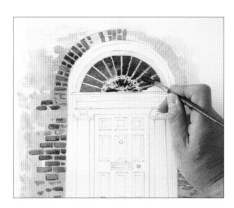

14 Add burnt umber to the ultramarine and paint the rest of the window while the first wash is wet.

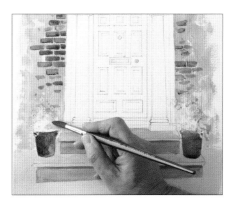

15 Paint the foliage in the pots with the no. 12 round and green gold.

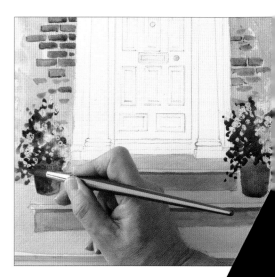

16 Mix a darker green from permanent sap green and burnt sienna and dab this in to the first wash wet into wet.

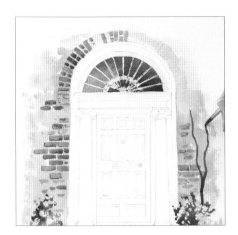

17 Paint the stem of the ivy on the wall with burnt umber and olive green.

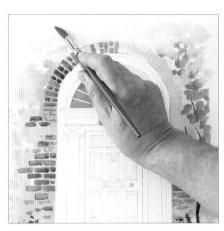

18 Begin to paint the foliage of the ivy with the no. 12 brush and green gold.

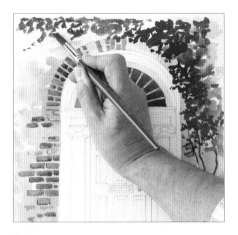

19 Paint the darker parts of the foliage wet into wet with Hooker's green and burnt umber.

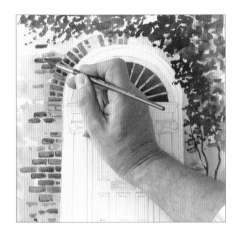

20 Add a few more bricks with burnt sienna.

21 Paint the shaded parts of the white paintwork around the window with cobalt blue and burnt sienna, then drop in a darker mix at the top of the arch, wet into wet.

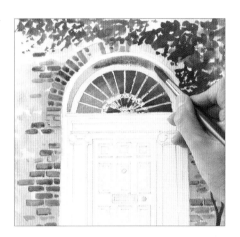

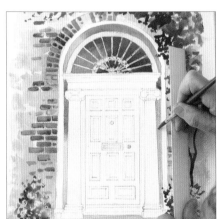

22 Use the no. 8 brush with a ruler and the same colours to paint the white paintwork at the sides of the pillars. Paint the lighter mix first, ˥ drop in the darker one.

˥t for the shaded
˥ sides of the
. Allow to dry.

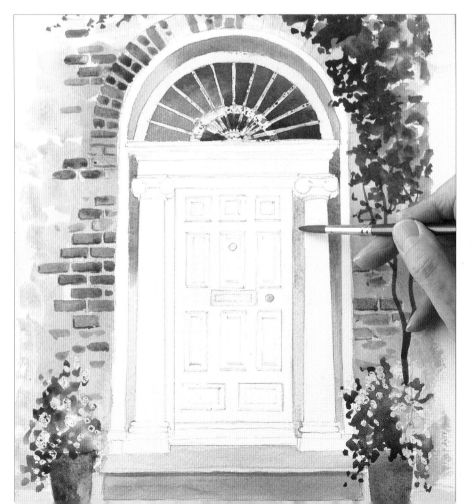

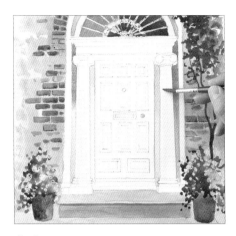

24 To paint the columns, wet a column with the no. 8 brush and clean water, then run a thin wash of cobalt blue down the left-hand side. Repeat for the other column. Allow to dry.

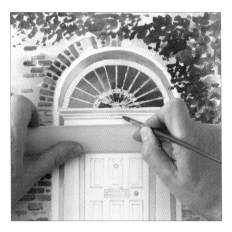

25 Paint the paintwork above the door with the same colour, using a ruler to help you.

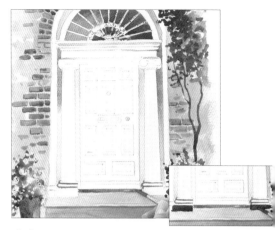

26 Use a darker mix of the same colours to paint details at the bottom of the pillars and the dark line under the door. Paint the black bases of the columns with ultramarine and burnt umber.

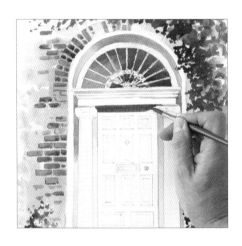

27 Paint the underside of the porch with cobalt blue, burnt sienna and a touch of cadmium red. Allow to dry.

28 Use the no. 12 brush and cadmium red to paint the door. Use the ruler to help with straight edges.

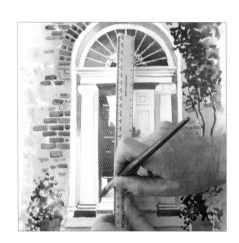

29 While the first wash is wet, drop in ultramarine at the top of the door to create shadow. Allow to dry.

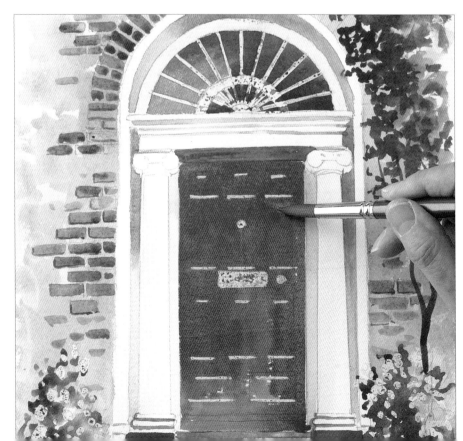

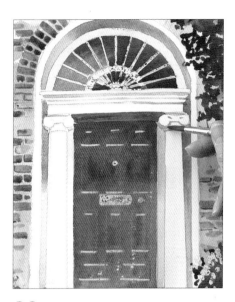

30 Paint details at the top of the columns with the no. 8 brush and burnt sienna with ultramarine.

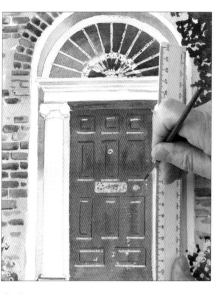

31 Use the no. 4 brush with a mix of ultramarine and cadmium red and a ruler to paint the darker details on the door.

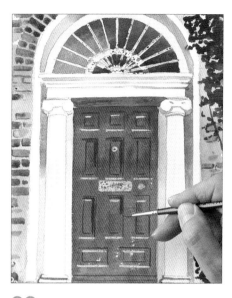

32 Put some more red into the door panels with cadmium red. Allow to dry.

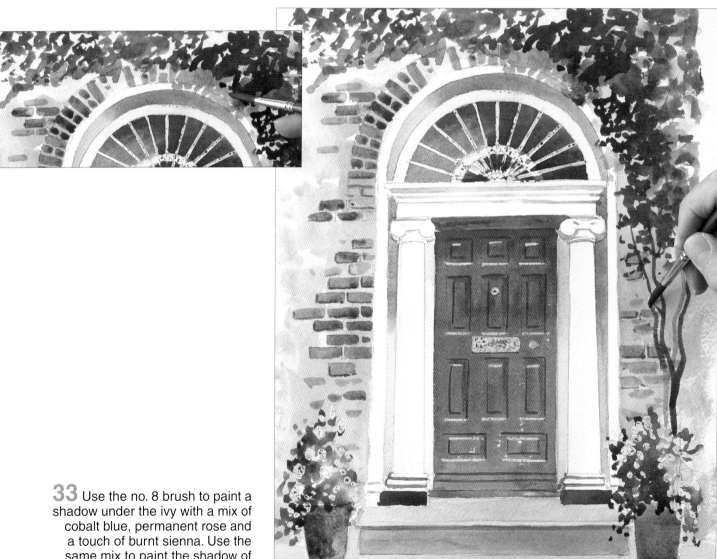

33 Use the no. 8 brush to paint a shadow under the ivy with a mix of cobalt blue, permanent rose and a touch of burnt sienna. Use the same mix to paint the shadow of the ivy stem.

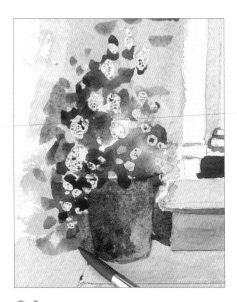

34 Use the same mix to add shade around the pot plants. Allow to dry.

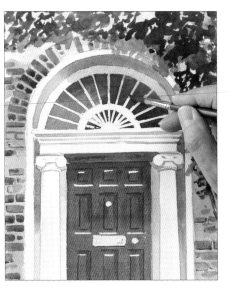

35 Remove the masking fluid with clean fingers. Use the no. 8 brush and cobalt blue with burnt sienna to shade areas of the window frame.

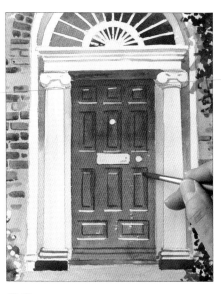

36 Using a very pale wash of cadmium red, go over the white areas left by the masking fluid.

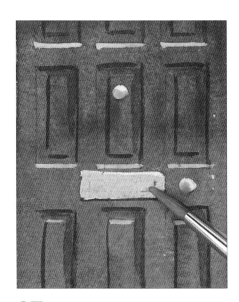

37 Paint the brass doorknobs and the letter box with raw sienna.

38 While the raw sienna wash is wet, drop in cobalt blue.

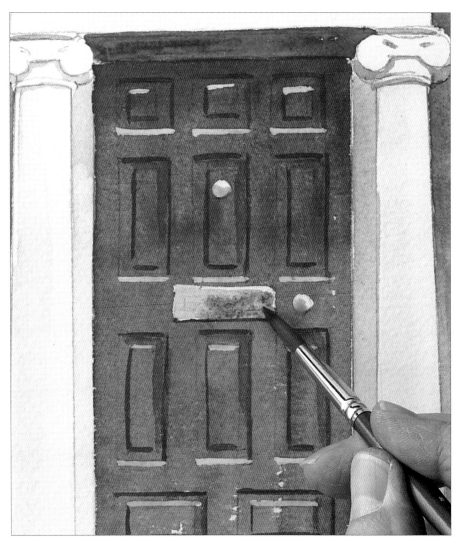

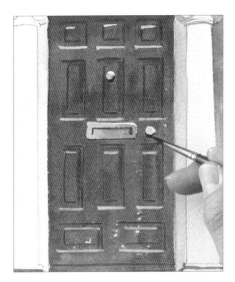

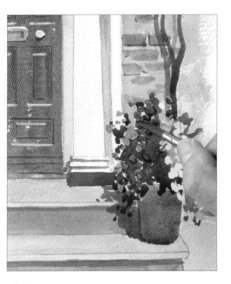

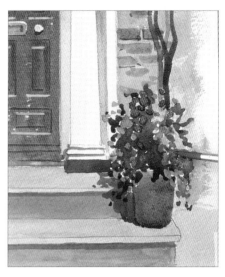

39 Paint the dark details on the brass door ornaments with the no. 4 brush and ultramarine with burnt umber.

40 Paint the flowers in the left of the right-hand pot with the no. 8 brush and permanent rose.

41 Add cobalt blue to the mix to paint the flowers on the right.

42 Paint some pink flowers in the left-hand pot, then add shade to the white flowers with a wash of cobalt blue.

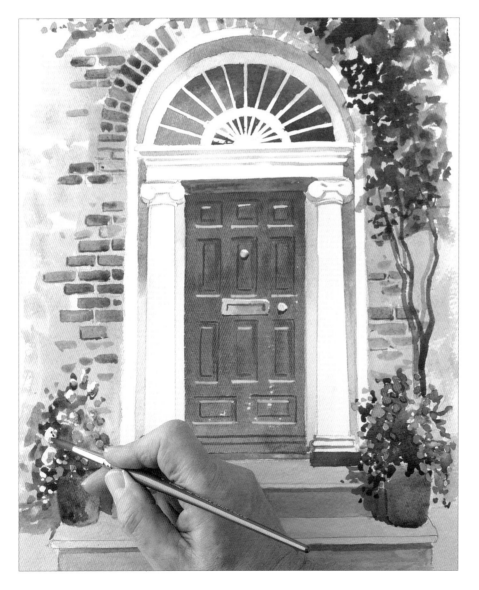

Opposite

The finished painting, shown reduced in size.

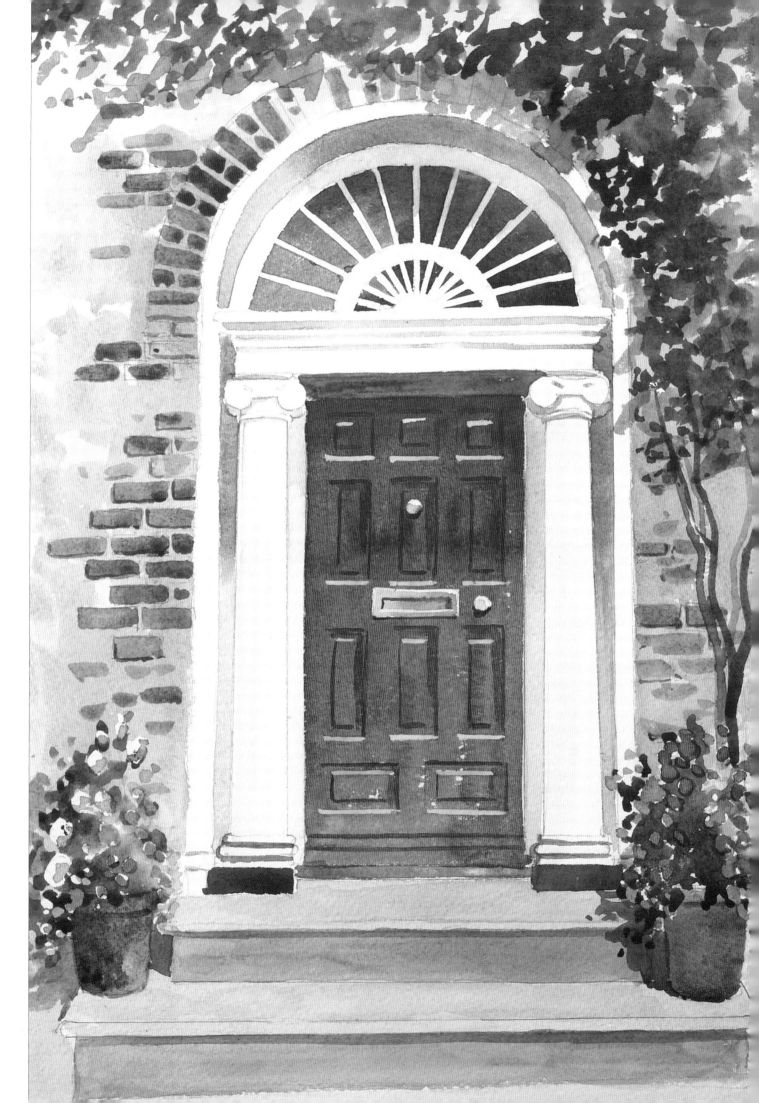

Index

The Mountains of Mourne, County Down
43 x 31cm (17 x 12¼in)

The Mourne Mountains, a granite range located in County Down in the south-east of Northern Ireland, are the country's most famous mountains. They are surrounded by outstanding natural beauty and are a real inspiration for writers, poets and artists like me.

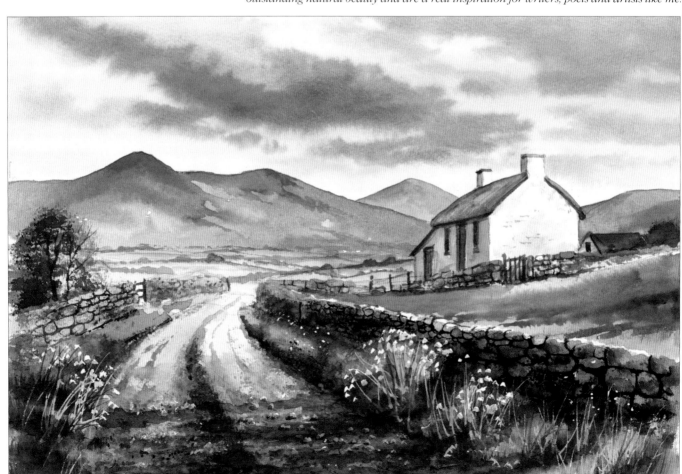